Yankee Doodle Dandy

# Yankee Doodle Dandy

*Edited with an introduction by*

## Patrick McGilligan

*Published for the Wisconsin Center for Film and Theater Research by*
*The University of Wisconsin Press*

Published 1981

The University of Wisconsin Press
114 North Murray Street
Madison, Wisconsin 53715

The University of Wisconsin Press, Ltd.
1 Gower Street
London WC1E 6HA England

First printing

Printed in the United States of America

For LC CIP information see the colophon

ISBN 0-299-08470-1 cloth; 0-299-08474-4 paper

Publication of this volume has been assisted by a grant from
The Brittingham Fund, Inc.

# Contents

# Foreword

*In donating the Warner Film Library* to the Wisconsin Center
for Film and Theater Research in 1969, along with the RKO and
Monogram film libraries and UA corporate records, United Artists created a truly great resource for the study of American
film. Acquired by United Artists in 1957, during a period when
the major studios sold off their films for use on television, the
Warner library is by far the richest portion of the gift, containing
eight hundred sound features, fifteen hundred short subjects,
nineteen thousand still negatives, legal files, and press books,
in addition to screenplays for the bulk of the Warner Brothers
product from 1930 to 1950. For the purposes of this project, the
company has granted the Center whatever publication rights it
holds to the Warner films. In so doing, UA has provided the
Center another opportunity to advance the cause of film schol-
arship.

Our goal in publishing these Warner Brothers screenplays is
to explicate the art of screenwriting during the thirties and forties, the so-called Golden Age of Hollywood. In preparing a
critical introduction and annotating the screenplay, the editor of
each volume is asked to cover such topics as the development
of the screenplay from its source to the final shooting script,
differences between the final shooting script and the release
print, production information, exploitation and critical reception of the film, its historical importance, its directorial style,
and its position within the genre. He is also encouraged to go
beyond these guidelines to incorporate supplemental information concerning the studio system of motion picture production.

We could set such an ambitious goal because of the richness
of the script files in the Warner Film Library. For many film titles, the files might contain the property (novel, play, short
story, or original story idea), research materials, variant drafts

of scripts (from story outline to treatment to shooting script), post-production items such as press books and dialogue continuities, and legal records (details of the acquisition of the property, copyright registration, and contracts with actors and directors). Editors of the Wisconsin/Warner Bros. Screenplay Series receive copies of all the materials, along with prints of the films (the most authoritative ones available for reference purposes), to use in preparing the introductions and annotating the final shooting scripts.

In the process of preparing the screenplays for publication, typographical errors were corrected, punctuation and capitalization were modernized, and the format was redesigned to facilitate readability.

Unless otherwise specified, the photographs are frame enlargements taken from a 35-mm print of the film provided by United Artists.

In 1977 Warner Brothers donated the company's production records and distribution records to the University of Southern California and Princeton University, respectively. These materials are now available to researchers and complement the contents of the Warner Film Library donated to the Center by United Artists.

*Tino Balio*
*General Editor*

*George M. Cohan, 1941*

# Introduction
## "The Life Daddy Would Have Liked to Live"

### Patrick McGilligan

*In the United States* of post–World War II, sobered as a nation by the experiences of the Vietnam war and Watergate, *Yankee Doodle Dandy* may seem almost like a foreign movie in its blithe patriotic delirium, or like a rose-colored capsule of time, for that is what it so perfectly is. Yet if *Dandy* is no longer quite as convincing a celebration of Americana as it must have been for audiences of the forties, it is no less enjoyable today for its richness as entertainment. The screen version of George M. Cohan's life story may not have a solid grasp on truth of fact or history—actually, it is more of a fairy tale than a faithful biography—but it is nonetheless an enduring classic of the musical genre. It has a secure niche in circulation among revival movie houses, and it pops up annually on television on the Fourth of July, a perennial favorite of buffs and general audiences alike.

The making of *Dandy* offers one of those fascinating and complicated tales that illustrates so well the machinations of Hollywood, off the screen as well as on.

Cohan's life was a natural subject for the movies and one that was well timed in its flag-waving appeal with the threat of global war on the horizon in 1941. In his heyday, Cohan had been, in the words of Walter Winchell, "Mr. Broadway." George Jean Nathan called him "America's first actor." Author of some 35 to 40 plays, the star or financial backer of some 125 other attractions, Cohan dominated the American musical theater in the early twentieth century. His present-day reputation is somewhat in eclipse. Much of his material has dated poorly, and he has been outlived by the detractors he cultivated during an often stormy career.[1] Though *George M!*, a loose-knit musical about his life, opened a modest run on Broadway in 1969, only a handful of Cohan's five hundred songs are widely known or sung nowadays, being limited mainly to those included in the *Dandy* score, among them "Mary," "You're a Grand Old Flag," "Give My Regards to Broadway," and "Yankee Doodle Dandy." Yet his importance goes beyond any vogue. In his lifetime as now, Cohan symbolized in his career the passing of the dying tradition of vaudeville and the transition to the emerging world of the American musical play.

It is ironic, then, that Cohan's legacy is upheld by a motion picture, because Cohan himself, during his lifetime, had an ambivalent relationship with movies. Though his plays were the basis for at least twenty-five films, he appeared in few of them.[2] His silent credits include appearances in three long-forgotten titles: *Broadway Jones* (1917), the first of several screen renditions of *Seven Keys to Baldpate* (1917), and *Hit-the-Trail Holliday* (1918), a farce about a Billy Sunday-type reformed bartender that was written expressly for brother-in-law Fred Niblo, Jr., a vaudevillian turned movie director. But silent movies could not capture the vivid essence of Cohan's personal flamboyance and animated delivery, and by the time talkies arrived, his career had already peaked. Cohan was not much in demand in Hollywood. He did manage to star in two early talking pictures, however, *The Phantom President* and *Gambling*, which, from all

1. Composer Richard Rodgers, for example, was among Cohan's detractors. Rodgers clashed with the headstrong Cohan during the shooting of *The Phantom President* as well as during the stage production of *I'd Rather Be Right*, both Rodgers-Hart scores. In his autobiography, *Musical Stages* (New York: Random House, 1975), Rodgers described Cohan's shows as simple-minded and corny, adding that "as a composer he was hardly up there with the Kerns, Berlins or Gershwins" (p. 154).

2. Among the motion pictures based on Cohan story material are *A Prince There Was* (1921), *Get-Rich-Quick Wallingford* (1921), *Little Johnny Jones* (1923), *Seven Keys to Baldpate* (1925, 1929, and 1935), *The Song and Dance Man* (1926 and 1936), *The Home Towners* (1928), *The Broadway Melody* (1929), *The Cock-eyed World* (1929), *Fast Company* (1929), *The Miracle Man* (1929), *Elmer the Great* (1933), *Times Square Playboy* (1936), *Ladies Must Live* (1940), and *Little Nellie Kelly* (1940).

accounts, were calamitous experiences for the aging trouper.

It was producer Jesse M. Lasky who reportedly convinced Cohan to appear in Paramount's *The Phantom President* in 1932, a presidential election year. The script, about a traveling medicine showman who is a dead ringer for a dull presidential candidate, had seeming topical merit; the tunes were by Richard Rodgers and Lorenz Hart, then under contract in Hollywood. Cohan supposedly had a gentleman's agreement with Lasky to tinker with the script and songs. But Cohan's arrival "coincided with the eruption of a major power struggle among Paramount executives, and Cohan's friends in the studio lost. The emergent powers regarded the Cohan contract as something they would have to suffer through."[3] Cohan's motorcar was halted at the studio gates—only bona fide movie stars were granted a drive-on. He feuded with Rodgers and Hart. His suggestions for revising the screenplay were rejected. His fame was exploited for cheap publicity purposes, and when, at one point, he sang one of the movie's ditties, "The Country Needs a Man," before the civic-minded Los Angeles Breakfast Club, his treatment was humiliating. "The initiation," according to *The Phantom President*'s publicist, who is quoted in John McCabe's *George M. Cohan*, "consisted of this leading figure in theatrical history sitting blindfolded on a wooden horse and taking an oath while a chortling baldie held Cohan's palm pressed upon a platter of sunny-side-up eggs and greasy ham." Unsurprisingly, Cohan's ordeal at Paramount encouraged his disdain of picture-making. When he left Hollywood, he gave interviews to the press saying that he would rather have spent a vacation in prison at Leavenworth.

The movie, which heralded in its crawl Cohan's "first appearance on the talking screen," is rarely viewed nowadays; occasionally it is shown on late-night television. Directed by Norman Taurog, with a cast that includes a youthful Claudette Colbert and comedian Jimmy Durante, *The Phantom President* is ambitious in its musical construction, comic "lookalike" theme,

---

3. John McCabe, *George M. Cohan: The Man Who Owned Broadway* (New York: Doubleday, 1973), p. 219. This account of the filming of *The Phantom President* is drawn largely from McCabe's book.

and political satire; unfortunately, it is also stagey and slow. Yet, as Cohan's only musical performance in movies, it provides an opportunity to study his characteristic style—the twisted smile, the catlike tread, the jaunty manner. In *Gambling* (1934), directed by Rowland V. Lee for Fox and adapted by Garrett Graham from Cohan's own nonmusical play, Cohan played the operator of a ritzy nightclub whose adopted daughter is mysteriously murdered. But he did not return to Hollywood for the production; *Gambling* was shot on Long Island. And it proved no more popular with audiences or critics than *The Phantom President*. Hence Cohan's film career appeared to be ended.

By the advent of the forties, Cohan, inactive and rumored to be seriously ill with cancer, was eager to promote and preserve his fame. In December 1939 he acted as consultant to a play about his life in the theater called *Yankee Doodle Boy*, written by Walter Kerr (later the New York drama critic) and Leo Brady and presented by the Harlequin Club of Catholic University in Washington, D.C. One of the early attempts to tell a composer-performer's biography through his or her music, *Yankee Doodle Boy* was evidently a popular stage production. It revived Cohan's off-and-on desire to sell his life story to a Hollywood studio;[4] understanding the lasting glamour of movies, "he was aware that this was a valuable property, and he wanted it done with style and taste."[5] First, Cohan reportedly took his ideas to

4. At least one Hollywood studio (Paramount) expressed interest in the film rights to *Yankee Doodle Boy* (Warner Brothers to Walter Kerr, December 13, 1939, Walter Kerr Collection, Wisconsin Center for Film and Theater Research, Madison, Wis.).

5. James Cagney, *Cagney by Cagney* (New York: Doubleday, 1976), p. 104.

Though there is evidence to the contrary, Robert Buckner disputes the stories about Cohan's shopping the life rights to his biography around Hollywood. "Mr. Cohan had not put his life story on the market," according to the screenwriter. "It was the idea of Jack L. Warner, who for many years was a Cohan admirer, and who learned that Cohan might be approachable, with sufficient tact, but who also had great misgivings about Hollywood's notorious liberties with lives of its film subjects. Cohan had had some bad experience with Paramount Studios in the past with one of his play properties, and was a 'burnt child' as a result. A very wealthy man still, he did not need the money for the rights to his life story, nor did his ego prod him. He simply had to be convinced that his life

producer Samuel Goldwyn, who tentatively commited himself to a version of Cohan's story starring Fred Astaire. Astaire balked, thinking the role not quite right for himself. Then Cohan took his story to Paramount, eventually refusing their offer. At some point in the process, Cohan turned to his longtime confidant Edward J. MacNamara for advice. MacNamara, a character actor who had once appeared in Cohan's shows, was also a close friend of James Cagney. MacNamara reminded Cohan that Cagney, the quintessential movie "tough guy," was an expert song-and-dance man too.

Cohan and Cagney were drawn together by converging motives at this particular point in history, although Cohan may not have been aware of this at the time. Cagney had political motives: twice since arriving in Hollywood he had been publicly accused of being a member of the Communist Party. In 1934 Cagney was wrongly accused by a Sacramento grand jury. In 1940 the then left-liberal Cagney was labeled a Communist by another grand jury, and the charge was repeated by Buron Fitts, a fellow who was campaigning for reelection as the district attorney of Los Angeles. The Sacramento accusations were dropped, and Fitts lost his race, but the "smear" on Cagney's politics lingered in the public consciousness. According to the *New York Times* (January 10, 1943), Cagney's brother "William Cagney[6] [the associate producer of *Dandy*] then enlisted the aid

---

was in friendly hands, that his fullest approval of every line of the script was assured. Jack Warner knew this when he sent for me and confided the problem before sending me to New York to work on-and-with Cohan to secure his consent" (Buckner to McGilligan, August 7, 1980).

6. The younger brother of James Cagney, William Cagney was a slightly heavier lookalike who had his own fleeting career as an actor in the early thirties. He had roles in *Ace of Aces* (1933), *Lost in the Stratosphere* (1934), *Palooka* (1934), *Flirting with Danger* (1934), *Stolen Harmony* (1934), and a cameo in the Cagney Productions' *Kiss Tomorrow Goodbye* (1950). By the forties, William Cagney had quit acting and emerged as brother James's closest career adviser. Starting with *Torrid Zone* (1940), he was associate producer on all of James Cagney's movies at Warner Brothers leading up to *Dandy*. Though his name did not appear as supervisor on the *Dandy* screenplay until the Temporary script (October 16, 1941), ostensibly Buckner's fourth draft, it is likely that he took an increasing role in the project, ultimately handling the day-to-day development for the producer of

of Congressman Martin Dies, who, not loath to join the controversy, investigated James and pronounced him, unequivocally, a sound citizen. But even so, the Cagneys were tired of political labels. So William went to Warner Brothers and said to J. L. Warner, 'There's one more thing to do. We should make a movie with Jim playing the damndest patriotic man in the country.' Warner asked who. Cagney said: George M. Cohan."

In due order, a thirty-nine-page contract was drawn up between Cohan and Warner Brothers. The contract awarded Cohan $125,000 and ten per cent of the "total gross receipts" of *Yankee Doodle Dandy* in exchange for his life story. (According to a 1956 report in *Variety*, Cagney got ten per cent of the "total gross receipts" as well.) "Said photoplay," the contract noted, "shall be of not less than six thousand (6000) lineal feet in length, and shall be first class in every respect and shall be made under the personal supervision of Mr. Jack L. Warner." Cohan got approval of title or subtitle as well as "final decision in connection with the characterizations, dialogue and all references to the characters of Helen F. Cohan, Jerry J. Cohan, Josephine Cohan and George M. Cohan, individually and in their associations with the American theatre." In the event of Cohan's unavailability or death, approval or disapproval of *Dandy* would revert to Cohan's lifelong lawyer-friend, Dennis F. O'Brien. For its part, Warners received LP rights, 16-mm film rights, and radio rights and television rights ("or any process analogous thereto now known or hereinafter devised"), in addition to life rights.

As part of the agreement, Cohan consented to provide material for a *Dandy* script "which may be wholly or partly fictional, as finally edited and approved by Mr. Cohan." Cohan also agreed to provide music and piano arrangements. The contract stipulated that there would be "no songs or musical compositions, or parts of same, [which] shall be used in the aforesaid

---

record, Hal B. Wallis. After *Dandy*, the Cagney brothers left Warners and launched one of Hollywood's more interesting independent film outfits, the short-lived Cagney Productions. See Patrick McGilligan's *Cagney: The Actor as Auteur* (South Brunswick, N.J.: A. S. Barnes, 1975) for additional background on the career relationship between the Cagney brothers.

photoplay except those written and composed by Mr. Cohan and Mr. Cohan agrees to originate, compose and write three new additional songs (including the words and music thereof), which shall be herein referred to as 'New Musical Compositions.'"[7] Finally, in a clause that was unusual for such movie contracts, the Cohan-Warners pact stipulated plainly that the star of the intended motion picture would be James Cagney, "who, it is agreed, is an actor possessing unique and extraordinary ability and is well and favorably known as such in all parts of the world, where motion picture photoplays in which James Cagney has heretofore appeared, have been exhibited."

## In the Beginning

The screenwriter who was assigned to the Cohan story, under veteran Warners producer Hal B. Wallis, was seemingly an odd choice: Robert Buckner.[8] There is little in Buckner's career to suggest either a musical inclination or a special affinity for the

7. The "three new additional songs" required from Cohan by contract were evidently never written for *Dandy*. And at least two non-Cohan songs were incorporated into the score, violating the clause specifying that "no songs or musical compositions" be used for *Dandy* except those composed by Cohan. One of the songs is just a snatch of "All Aboard for Old Broadway" by Jack Scholl and M. K. Jerome. The other is the entirety of "Off the Record" from the Broadway play *I'd Rather Be Right* by Cohan's old adversaries, Rodgers and Hart. That song was purchased outright from Rodgers and Hart and playwrights George S. Kaufman and Moss Hart (no relation) for two thousand dollars. Although Cohan obviously was not able to keep the Rodgers-Hart song out of the eventual score, he did get a revenge of sorts. The song and its composers are not credited anywhere in the picture or its publicity.

8. Hal Wallis, an able, veteran producer with a long list of distinguished credits, was associated with Warner Brothers during the studio's heyday as a studio boss and "house producer" (and later, after he left Warners, as an "independent" under contract to Paramount and Universal). *Dandy* is one of ten pictures he is credited with producing for Warners in 1942. Considering William Cagney's involvement as "associate producer," it is interesting to note that it was common practice for the studio, in the thirties and early forties, to credit higher-up executives (even, in some instances, Jack Warner himself) as being "producer" of a particular picture. It wasn't until mid-1942 that Warners production supervisors, known as associate producers since 1938, were finally awarded their deserved title of producer. This suggests that William Cagney's participation as "associate

Cohan story. Of English and Scottish descent, Buckner was born on a plantation near Richmond, Virginia. Before arriving in Hollywood in the late 1930s, he wrote fiction and articles for *Collier's*, *The New Yorker*, *Redbook*, *Atlantic Monthly*, *Vanity Fair*, *Cosmopolitan*, *Harper's Bazaar*, and *Esquire*. He had been a foreign correspondent, written humor for *Punch*, published short stories and travelogues, and written a novel in England. A screenwriter whose contract with Warner Brothers spanned the for-

---

producer" became increasingly significant as the production of *Dandy* developed.

Of star James Cagney, Wallis writes revealingly in his autobiography, "He [Cagney] and I never became friends. He was cold to me, and I wasn't particularly fond of him" (Hal Wallis and Charles Higham, *Starmaker: The Autobiography of Hal Wallis* [New York: Macmillan, 1980], p. 49). Likewise, Wallis gets scant mention in Cagney's autobiography. On the other hand, Buckner lauds the producer's contributions: "My relations with Hal Wallis were good. I had written several successful films for Warner Brothers, and he and Jack had discussed several producers and writers before assigning anyone. . . . Neither Wallis, Warner nor Bill Cagney interfered with me when I wrote the full treatment, or plan, for the first draft of the screenplay. Mainly because they then knew that I had Cohan's complete confidence, and that what I wrote had his approval. Wallis was most helpful and wise in working with me or advising me on certain matters in this first draft" (Buckner to McGilligan, August 7, 1980).

Thus, from the outset, it appears there were two camps aligned against each other over crucial production decisions—Wallis and Buckner of one mind, the Cagneys of another. The history of the production suggests that the Cagneys, using James's box-office bargaining clout, ultimately got the upper hand and usurped prerogatives in some areas as the making of *Dandy* progressed.

Buckner adds a provocative parenthetical note explaining his assignment to the Cohan story: "There was something a little more to it, that's never been aired until now. Cohan had some anti-Semitic prejudices to combine with his Hollywood ones, and he had reasons that he explained to me during the three months or so that I worked with him in New York. He was also a solid Catholic, if occasionally lapsing, and he liked the screenplay I wrote on the life of Knute Rockne of Notre Dame. This, together with the fact that I am a Gentile, was, I believe, the determining factor in my selection. I had never written a musical nor was I old enough to have seen Cohan on the stage. There was a great difference in our ages but we had a good rapport from the start. He was a lonely man at the time, with a short time to live, and aware of it. After the film's release and success he wrote me a beautiful letter of thanks and congratulations" (Buckner to McGilligan, August 7, 1980).

ties, Buckner wrote or cowrote numerous pictures during his career, including *Gold Is Where You Find It* (1938), *Love, Honor, and Behave* (1938), *Comet over Broadway* (1938), *The Oklahoma Kid* (1939), *You Can't Get Away with Murder* (1939), *Dodge City* (1939), *Angels Wash Their Faces* (1939), *Virginia City* (1940), *Santa Fe Trail* (1940), *My Love Came Back* (1940), *Dive Bomber* (1941), *Confidential Agent* (1945), *Rogue's Regiment* (1948), *Sword in the Desert* (1949), *Deported* (1950), *Bright Victory* (1951), *To Paris with Love* (1955), *A Prize of Gold* (1955), *Love Me Tender* (1956), *Triple Deception* (1957), and *From Hell to Texas* (1958). His credits as a producer include *Gentleman Jim* (1942), *Mission to Moscow* (1943), *The Desert Song* (1943), and *Life with Father* (1947). At the time of his assignment to *Dandy*, Buckner had just completed writing another successful screen biography for Warners, *Knute Rockne—All American* (1940).

Buckner took his assignment to heart and plunged into the research. His source material included a scrapbook of clippings about Cohan's stage career (including a batch of essays penned by the prodigious Cohan), critical notices, newspaper gossip items, and in-depth magazine profiles, as well as Cohan's own autobiography (which was designated by the contract as an essential reference), *Twenty Years on Broadway and the Years It Took to Get There* (Harper, 1924). But Buckner's primary source, as stipulated by the contract, was to be Cohan himself. A Warners press release (dated April 2, 1941), which was duly published in *Variety*, announced that "Cohan will come to Hollywood soon to confer on production plans for the picture. All material to be used will be compiled by Cohan and transcribed for the screen by Robert Buckner. Cohan will also supervise the production." Yet Cohan's advancing illness, and his distaste for the film capital, kept him in New York. Instead, Buckner was obliged to travel east for talks with Cohan's erstwhile director since 1910, Sam Forrest, with ex-partner Sam Harris, and with Cohan himself. These conversations provided the groundwork for Buckner's early drafts. Cohan took a fortuitous liking to Buckner, and vice versa. The aging song-and-dance master began to establish some guidelines for their collaboration.

According to Cagney, Cohan "specified a long list of taboos" in these initial meetings with Buckner. Among other things, Cohan insisted that there be no explicit love scenes in *Dandy* (Cohan had a prudery about screen romance) and that there be no mention whatsoever of his having been married twice. Specifically, there was to be no allusion to his first wife, Ethel Levey, a vaudeville headliner who quit as Cohan's leading lady after their divorce and subsequently became a popular musical comedy star in London. The former Mrs. Cohan was said to be eyeing the preparations for *Dandy* with mounting anxiety, for she and Cohan had split acrimoniously in 1907 when Cohan's amorous attentions were engaged by Agnes Mary Nolan, a chorus girl who had been a member of his company for three years. (Cohan married Agnes Mary Nolan, described by the *New York Telegraph* as "petite, pretty and dark-eyed," in June of 1907. Agnes Nolan's sister, Alice, later married Cohan's partner, Sam Harris.) Cohan's ban on love scenes was fine with Cagney. "This taboo on love scenes didn't bother me," the actor later recalled, "for the way I do a love scene, it's never a necking party. To me, a panting and grappling love scene is embarrassing when I see it on the screen. So when I sang 'Mary' to the girl who played Cohan's wife, I just told her the lyrics as she played the melody. I poured coffee, put sugar into it, stirred it and handed it to her. Then I sat down, drank the coffee, and she sang the lyric back to me. The way we did it, it was an effective love scene—without any lashings of goo!"[9] (see figure 16).

The transcript of these conversations between Buckner and Cohan indicates just how deeply Cohan influenced the story

9. James Cagney as told to Pete Martin, "How I Got This Way," *Saturday Evening Post*, January 14, 1956, p. 45.

Though Cagney's reminiscences and the script notes suggest otherwise, Buckner disputes that Cohan set tasteful parameters about his romantic life: "Cohan's main 'taboo', as you put it, was with the life and name of Ethel Levey, the wife with whom he still had bitter relations. He had no 'prudery' about romantic relations on the screen, being a very practical showman always, but he was insistent that the girl in our script be given the anonymous name of 'Mary',

line of *Dandy*.[10] Cohan's anecdotes about his childhood and youth were adopted wholesale for the vaudeville montage and "time-passing" sequences, for example —his birth in Providence, Rhode Island, on July 4, 1878, during a vaudeville stopover; his boyhood specialty of tap-dancing while playing a violin over his head (see figure 3); his riding of a donkey in a Wild West parade; his scuffling with townies after a too-persuasive performance as "Peck's Bad Boy" (the scene occurs almost ver-

---

and this satisfied everyone else as well (except Ethel Levey)." Buckner adds, "Cohan was responsible for most, if not all, of these changes in the romantic line of the story. He was being sued heavily at the time by Ethel Levey, as I recall, who had somehow gotten hold of an early script, or had been told about it by some of her friends in Hollywood, and was threatening George with all kinds of trouble. So if sweetness and light [in the romantic angle] did finally emerge it had other good reasons than a 'happy ending'" (Buckner to McGilligan, August 7, 1980).

10. The transcript is part of Buckner's research notes, the first item listed in the Inventory.

Buckner sheds further light on Cohan's input: "Cohan did not come to Hollywood during the film's production. He hated the place. On some points of fact in the production I believe he was consulted by the music, wardrobe and location departments of the studio, but all [the] while he remained in New York. . . .

"Cohan and I got along very well indeed. Every morning I went to his apartment on Fifth Avenue in New York, where we worked for anywhere from two to five hours, then took a long walk around the reservoir, often with 'Bugs' Baer, his old friend; and Cohan couldn't have been more cooperative. Many times he'd invite his old Broadway pals to join us, such ones as his ex-partner Sam Harris, and they'd sing and dance out some of their old routines for me, as well as tell me many incidents of their old days in the theatre. It was a great experience for any writer. . . .

"I met with Cohan daily for months in New York, and exchanged several letters with him later with regard to the various versions and changes of the scripts. His suggestions and contributions were always helpful, usually inserted or modified, and always presented politely. His own version of the story [see Inventory] did not influence me materially, but I respected it somewhat as a matter of diplomacy. He did not understand screenplay demands very well, or the technology of film production. His writing was naturally old-fashioned, his dialogue often badly dated, and understandably he did not see himself as objectively as he might have. I can't recall that he ever stiffly 'demanded' anything" (Buckner to McGilligan, August 7, 1980).

batim in the Kerr-Brady stage adaptation of Cohan's life story). Excerpts from the transcript show how Cohan provided the inspiration for the first third of Buckner's eventual first draft:

*1887*: That was when I made my first appearance on the stage as a violinist. I wore a silk suit—and played the violin not only with the bow, but juggled with it, threw it up over my head—
*1889–1891*: I rode a donkey with a wild west show—I was drum major at the head of the parade—my mother and sister were in a carriage throwing hand-bills.
*1891*: Atkinson engaged the family for "Peck's Bad Boy." This was the first character part I got—it was a real part—that was a big moment. All that season we played "Peck's Bad Boy." We played in Madison, Wisconsin, when Peck was Governor.
BUCKNER: You told me a story about the kids that waited for you in the alleys after the show—
COHAN: They would take a punch at me because I was Peck's bad boy—in those days everything was "Peck's Bad Boy." We played with that show all season—the next season we went to Buffalo for a two-weeks engagement, and stayed all season—we became the stock company.
*1895*: Gus Williams engaged us for the play "April Fool". (They didn't write in a part for me)—he saw us playing at the Central Music Hall, a summer theatre, and engaged us there. We just fitted in his play. We went with him for that season. That's when I got into a lot of trouble. I tried to tell him how to write his play. I had an awful time. My father had a tough time with me at that time.

Cohan's memory was virtually cinematic in some of its detail, as when he recalled the year 1917 for Buckner, evoking imagery that would later crop up in the movie:

Nothing much [that year] except the war song "Over There." I wrote it the morning we declared war. The idea occurred to me by the sound of the bugle call. I wrote the chorus and first verse coming over in the car and sent it over to Nora Bayes at the Maxine Elliot Theatre and she sang it that night, April 5, 1917 (check date). I don't remember the play she was doing at that time (check this). About a week afterwards, we went back to Fort Myer (some of these poor fellows never came back—in fact, 90 percent of them never came back). We had about a hundred acts for them—all the actors in New York wanted to go. We gave them a great show, and little Gus Edwards sang "Over There."[11] We taught the boys the chorus that night, and we all sang it together. Suddenly all the lights went out—we were in total darkness—everybody was scared to death—someone got the idea of turning on all the headlights of the trucks and cars parked outside and moved them up close to the barracks and we continued on with the show, with the headlights from the cars. It was the first time it was sung by a mob of people (meaning the song, "Over There").

The bugle call, the sea of Fort Myer recruits, the blackout, the headlights of trucks and cars—all are in *Dandy*. Cohan's elaborate reminiscences proved helpful also for the scenes between George and the president (the FDR figure played by Captain Jack Young), which were ultimately to form the framing device of Buckner's narrative (see figure 1).[12] Buckner asked Cohan about the Congressional Medal of Honor, awarded by Congress in 1936 to salute Cohan's meritorious service to the nation. According to the transcript, Cohan said:

That was given to me by Congress about 1935. I never had occasion to collect it until 1940. So it was in the president's desk for four years. They asked me many times to go down there—they wanted to make it a ceremonial thing—I was afraid it was too much of a publicity stunt, so I sneaked down myself one day—and got it. I had a long talk with the president, in the White House, in his office. He talked about the general condition abroad, and told me he was very much worried, but he realized what was going on. This was in 1940, about 7 or 8 months ago.

Q. He was quite familiar with your career.

A. He talked about having seen a lot of my plays—when I walked in, he said, "How is my double?" That was "I'd Rather Be Right."

11. Cohan's memory may have been playing tricks when he recollected the first public singing of "Over There." Accounts vary, but publicity attributes the first singing of "Over There" to Nora Bayes at Camp Merritt, Long Island, in 1917. Bayes is identified simply as "the singer" in *Dandy* and is played by Frances Langford.

12. I use the name George to refer to the character in the screenplay and film, and the name Cohan to refer to the man in real life.

Q. Would you have any objection to using that incident in the picture?
A. No.[13]

Of course, these remembered highlights of Cohan's lifetime underwent various dramatic permutations in the actual motion picture. Frances Langford and Cagney, rather than "little Gus Edwards," wound up singing "Over There," for example (see figure 24); history was manipulated so that the president's summoning George directly from a performance of *I'd Rather Be Right* coincides with the outbreak of World War II. And in some instances, Cohan's most cherished recollections were scrapped altogether in favor of more convenient drama; Cohan's embellished account of his first acquaintance with partner Sam Harris, for example, was ultimately dropped and instead fictionalized. But Cohan's autobiographical reflections provided Buckner with fertile material with which to begin his task, and Cohan's production photos and staging advice set the eventual musical numbers of *Dandy* in motion. Here, Buckner's assignment as screenwriter proved advisable, at least at the outset, for his training as a journalist would safeguard the authenticity of *Dandy* while the sprawling elements of Cohan's long and eventful career were being organized into story form.

### A Liberty with Facts

Six drafts of Buckner's *Dandy* script survive in the Warners files, although two of them are earmarked for Cohan's use and were evidently prepared simultaneously with the studio versions (with only slight revisions). Buckner's first draft began simply, with a "night shot" of George approaching the White House gates in a light drizzle of rain. Cohan's life story was then re-

13. Ironically, considering the staunch support of FDR reflected in Warner movies throughout the thirties and forties, *Dandy* included, Cohan actually disliked the New Deal president and his policies. According to Richard Rodgers in his autobiography, that is one of the reasons Cohan waited so long before collecting his Congressional Medal of Honor. Also, Cohan was notoriously anti-union and preferred the politics of his friend Alfred E. Smith. By the time Cohan finally met FDR, according to McCabe's book, "Roosevelt was at his most charming, and Cohan, who knew a lot about charm, was distinctly uncharmed, although he did not show it" (p. 248).

counted by him in flashback to the president. Thus the clever dramatic structure of *Dandy* was introduced right away, in the Screenplay and Outline (dated June 12–19, 1941) and the Revised Screenplay (June 23, 1941), the companion version sent to Cohan. In this scene between George and the president, Buckner found a device that neatly framed the rest of the unfolding story—Cohan's vaudeville training, his years on the road with the Four Cohans, his Broadway triumphs, his World War I activity on the home front, his retirement, his comeback in *I'd Rather Be Right*. There were many later revisions in Buckner's conceit, of course. Cohan is awarded his medal in this opening scene in the Screenplay and Outline, and he receives it in the closing scene of the Final script (November 25, 1941), five drafts later, a subtle but effective improvement in the structure. It wasn't until the Final script that a prologue was added to occur backstage after the opening night success of *I'd Rather Be Right*. But the symmetry of the opening and closing White House scenes was to be one of Buckner's principal contributions to the script whereby the strict chronology was artfully framed by the presidential visit.

It is clear in these first two drafts that Buckner was striving to be sincerely gracious and complimentary to Cohan. Not only did the screenwriter sprinkle his writing with generous asides about Cohan's character (Cohan is variously described as "remarkable," "amazing," "extremely likeable," and "every inch the professional"), but he also avoided depicting episodes in Cohan's career that were potentially embarrassing or unacceptable to him. No mention was made, for example, of Cohan's bitter experience in Hollywood or of the controversial and damaging role Cohan played during the Actor's Equity strike of 1919.[14] Josie was married off early in these drafts and then she

---

14. Buckner says, "There was no pressure put upon me to 'paint a rose-colored view of Cohan's life.' He told me more of the good than the bad, of course, as indeed what man or woman would not have done at his age? There was no sound professional reason for me to dig up the Actors' Equity Strike affair as a necessary element of the screenplay. I was 'running long' already with the good dramatic and musical elements, and needed to condense" (Buckner to McGilligan, August 7, 1980). See also footnote 10.

emigrated to Australia, following the desire of Cohan "to remove her gracefully from the rest of the story," according to notes that Buckner inserted in the script. The two Cohan wives were blended into one, a single character named Agnes, who springs from the chorus to befriend Cohan and is whimsically dubbed by him "Mary." This character, "though a minor element," Buckner noted in the script, "is vitally important for a warmth and interest in our personal story, and it requires a little freedom of scope from the actual facts; but it will be handled throughout in strict good taste, with nothing objectionable whatsoever. We are most anxious that Mr. Cohan will permit us this small liberty and will recognize its value to the picture. If desired, the girl's name can be made fictional."

The synopsis for the second half of Buckner's Screenplay and Outline (for at this stage in the development Buckner had written dialogue for only the first half of the movie) described the unexpectedly tragic twist that the screenwriter had in mind for the romance between George and Agnes. Agnes would denounce George because of his "high opinion" of himself, according to Buckner, and then leave him when he does not reciprocate her affections. "Deeply wounded," as much by the relentless carping of critics as by the desertion of Agnes, George attempts to write a serious play, *Popularity*. Agnes attends the play, unbeknownst to George, and happens to overhear the vi-

---

McCabe's book provides an excellent overview of the Equity strike, which changed the economic landscape of Broadway. When the Actor's Equity Association called a strike to protest intolerable working conditions in 1919, half the shows on Broadway were shut down. The four-week strike was bitter, with many big stars like the Barrymores, Al Jolson, Lillian Russell, Eddie Cantor, Marie Dressler, and Ed Wynn siding with Equity. Cohan, on the other hand, was instrumental in leading the Actor's Fidelity League, a counter-association sympathetic to the aims of producers. Actors denounced Cohan and sang a parody of "Over There," called "Over Fair," as a rallying call. The strike was won by Equity but Cohan never recognized the union, never joined its ranks, something for which he was never forgiven by many Equity members. "Were it not for this backsliding," McCabe quotes *Variety* editor Abel Green as saying, "Cohan today would still be the patron saint of all actors because he was the most versatile man on the American stage" (p. 156).

cious comments of reviewers during the show's intermission.[15] Then she leaves the theater in anguish and is swallowed up by the night. The synopsis noted: "What she as a woman saw clearly but helplessly as George's tragedy—the refusal of time to spare from public success for his own private happiness, an emotional blindness brought on by glamorous substitutes, the restless worker who never once pauses to look up from his make-believe world to grasp the worthwhile realities—in short, the tragedy of many a man—has finally caught up with him. And the simple things that she once held out to him along with her heart might have saved him. But the door was closed and she cannot re-open it."

Buckner's original synopsis continued in this maudlin vein. After the failure of *Popularity*, George becomes "the laughing-stock of the wise boys on Broadway," and the Cohan-Harris producing team hits the skids. A note in the script apologized for this "liberty with facts," adding, "We hope that Mr. Cohan will appreciate our dramatic reason—that continuous and mounting success, without even one break of failure, makes for a monotonous story. And since our story is principally one of character— the great ability of a man to pick himself up after a knock-down—the value of putting across this quality, without harm to anyone, seems reasonable and important." According to the synopsis, a down-on-his-luck George then encounters Agnes in a music store in 1917, just as she is playing a disc recording of "Give My Regards to Broadway" to a customer. Almost simultaneously, George is inspired by the notes of a bugle and composes the song "Over There." The song becomes hugely popular, he and Agnes are reunited (all the wiser for their misfortunes), and George's "genius" lights up the marquees of Broadway throughout the ensuing Roaring Twenties.

Curiously, one of the more stubborn wrinkles in the evolution of the script was to be the Cohan-Harris partnership. Harris, "native New Yorker, former newsboy, delivery man, and cough-

---

15. Among the remarks by critics (in the script) sure to rankle Cohan: "The play is cold as ice. There's no heart to it, no depth of emotion, especially in the women."

drop salesman,"[16] was Cohan's financial angel and long-time friend. In Buckner's first two drafts, they meet by chance while Harris is managing a lightweight prizefighter named "Terrible Terry" McGovern ("the famous little prizefighter of the 1900s, so-called because of the ferocious faces he made at his opponents in the ring," according to Buckner's script notes). McGovern is to be booked for a tour on the vaudeville circuit by producers Klaw and Erlanger, if he wins his championship bout with up-and-comer Gentleman Jim Corbett. But when Harris wagers the entire bankroll of Cohan's first production on McGovern, who loses, *Little Johnny Jones* nearly folds. George's career looks as if it has suffered one of those dramatic "knockdowns" so valued by Buckner, until the remaining three Cohans are summoned from the boondocks to perform without salary and rescue the show. Even though this intricate subplot had some basis in fact (Harris *was* the manager of "Terrible Terry" McGovern, who did lose the lightweight crown to young Corbett), Cohan was not interested in boxing as a sidelight to his own life story and correctly perceived it as a distraction. At Cohan's urging, the "Terrible Terry" subplot was gone by the second Revised Screenplay (September 30, 1941).[17]

Ultimately, Cohan's life was the theater and little else but the theater, and that is where the story had to center. Ironically, even in these first two drafts, Cohan's legitimate impact on the development of the American musical comedy (he deemphasized chorus girls, upgraded the plot, claimed to have introduced the royalty system for skits and revues) was given short shrift. There were only hints of Cohan's innovation, as in the scene in the Screenplay and Outline that takes place at the offices of Broadway entrepreneurs Marc Klaw and A. L. Erlanger.[18] The scene is described in symbolic terms by Buckner as

16. McCabe, *George M. Cohan*, p. 57.

17. Screenwriter Buckner evidently had a yen for the Gentleman Jim saga, which he satisfied after the success of *Dandy* when he graduated to associate producer status on Warners' 1942 period melodrama, *Gentleman Jim*.

18. Abraham Lincoln Erlanger, together with a succession of partners, virtually monopolized the pursestrings of turn-of-the-century American theater. He produced Cohan's *Forty-five Minutes from Broadway*. Erlanger survived as a bit character in the completed *Dandy*. His onetime partner, Marc Klaw, did not.

"the Old Theater facing the New." When George's new-fangled play is rejected by Erlanger, the producer upbraids him, "Don't you know you can't have a mob scene, shoot off guns, and play straight drama in a musical comedy?" A haughty actor who is also present, J. Medford Yates, joins the harangue by saying, "Young man, people do not converse that way in the legitimate theater. (He pauses, pursing his lips.) Your story is rather amusing in spots, but there is entirely too much else *between* the spots. No actor of standing would risk his reputation with such 'plain everyday talk.' (He leans forward slightly.) The theater, Mr. Cohan, is not Nature—but an improvement upon Nature." That pointed speech is whittled down in subsequent drafts and finally vanishes altogether.

## Getting Cohan's Approval

Buckner worked with haste over the summer of 1941, doubtless spurred on by Cohan's fading health and by Warners' own production imperatives. Cohan was anxious to have *Dandy* conform to his own vision, but he was also anxious to have the movie completed within his lifetime. At every stage of the project, consequently, Warners' front office fretted about getting Cohan's approval, although Cohan seemed to be cooperating with enthusiasm. Buckner was in regular contact with Cohan and may have journeyed to New York on at least one other occasion that summer to keep Cohan abreast of the quickening developments. The second Revised Screenplay was still not completed; the second part of *Dandy* existed in outline form only. In a memo (June 19, 1941) to producer Hal Wallis, Buckner emphasized the need to keep Cohan apprised:

Dear Hal:

Here is a detailed treatment on the last section of *Yankee Doodle Dandy*, as you requested.

I have written the important scenes with dialogue, so that both you and Mr. Cohan can get a clear idea of their contents; and also because it greatly simplifies my job with the screenplay.

I hope you can share my enthusiasm about the story. As you may recall, nobody was more worried about it than I. But now, in all sincerity, I think we have the set-up of a really great picture—with a fine theme, a lot of laughs and a tight story. At any rate I've worked like hell to make it like that.

Your idea of getting Cohan's approval at this point strikes me as being very sensible. Knowing his feelings on the subject, I believe he will try to meet us half-way. I have respected his objections wherever possible, but in the matter of the love story he may need a little subtle persuasion to let us retain it—even though there is nothing objectionable in it that I can see. And it is vital to the picture.

As we did at this stage of the Rockne picture, I think it would be a great saving in time and money if I could go thru the story personally with Cohan, rather than leave it wide open for him to shoot at alone. I could explain why every step was made, or make his fixes on the spot; get his definite approval much more easily than by a long and complicated correspondence. That might take weeks, during which most of my time would be lost. Getting Cohan's O.K. needs personal handling, I assure you. He's a peculiar old boy, and once he starts kicking it around with Wilk, Ebenstein or his lawyer O'Brien—the real grief will begin. But he seems to like me and I think we could iron out any wrinkles without much trouble.

There's no thought on my part to go to New York for any other reason but this. I'd much rather stay here and go fishing. But it will be a sure short-cut if you want to get Cohan's "go-ahead" for production this year.

Bob Buckner

## Cohan by Cohan

After reading the second Revised Screenplay, Cohan gave a tentative go-ahead for the production. Meanwhile, Cohan wrote his own two-hundred-page screenplay for *Dandy*, offering suggestions and revisions while roughly following the frame-flashback structure that Buckner had devised. The Cohan version survives (see Inventory), and it is an intriguing document. Prominent among his concerns were the musical staging, the accuracy of the chronology, and overall period authenticity. He suggested staging "So Long, Mary," for example, "as originally produced. It is not only one of the simplest and most effective numbers ever done in any music show, but has become sort of semi-classic." He offered to supply "the original dialogue for the Grocery Store scene from 'Peck's Bad Boy,'" adding, "The idea that you have in the script about a spotter being out in front (who represents the Keith Circuit) is all wrong for the simple reason that such spotters only attended Variety and Burlesque Shows and straight shows did not interest them. Not only that, but I should like to hold back all talk of vaudeville until 1893 when Keith first opened the Union Square Theatre." Cohan also objected to being linked with Klaw and Erlanger so conspicuously in Buckner's script, in view of his actual (marginal) ties with the two stage producers.

The visit to the White House also concerned Cohan greatly. Cohan complained in a script note, "To begin with, I don't like the idea of the midnight appointment with the President. To me, this is so far-fetched that I can't understand how anybody could possible believe it. And so I suggest that it be an 11 A.M. appointment, which it really was, and of course this will necessitate a new opening. Now mind you, I'm not telling you how to make this change. I'm merely offering a suggestion which may not be worth a nickel from the motion picture standpoint." Cohan also objected to the "colored butler" in the White House scene, noting authoritatively that he had visited the White House many times during his lifetime, especially during Woodrow Wilson's administration, "and I have never seen a colored butler there." (Lest this objection be interpreted as progressive thinking on Cohan's part, it should be noted that Cohan himself, the writer of many popular "coon songs," chose to end his version of the *Dandy* script with a racial stereotype, a patriotic "old darkey" taxi driver humming the melody of "Yankee Doodle Dandy.") Also, the president refers to Jerry Cohan as being an Irish immigrant in Buckner's Screenplay and Outline. In his script, Cohan proudly corrected that reference to "American-born."

The treatment of George's romance with Agnes was resolved in a priggish fashion in Cohan's script. Cohan simply ignored Agnes for most of the story line and then contrived an abrupt rendezvous between the characters of the ex-chorus girl and George at the end of the piece, after George has retired from the theater. According to the Cohan script, George is vacationing with his mother aboard an ocean liner when Agnes (accompanied by her aunt and uncle) fortuitously materializes; that leads to an extended (platonic) romantic spree in Europe, with both George and Agnes chaperoned by family. Both parents, Jerry and Nellie Cohan, figure far more prominently in Cohan's draft than the Agnes character, who really does not even enter into the proceedings until the final third of the story. Even Cohan's personal circle of friends fared better than the composite woman in his life. Cohan enlarged the parts Buckner had sketched into the synposis for director Sam Forrest, press agent Eddie Dunn, and lawyer-friend "Cap" O'Brien. Cohan even included a protracted flashback sequence of his first boyhood meeting with O'Brien in 1885.

Cohan also felt that the Cohan-Harris relationship needed a complete overhaul. According to the transcript of Cohan's recollections, the two future partners had met at a Sunday outing of the Words and Music Club on Staten Island in the spring of 1904. Thus, Cohan set his version of their first encounter during a ballgame (Words versus Music) at that picnic. Harris is brought in as a relief pitcher for the opposing team; actually he is a ringer, not a songwriter or a lyricist but the promoter-manager of "Terrible Terry" McGovern (who gets only a fleeting mention in the Cohan version). Harris pitches to George and strikes him out. Later, on the ferryboat back to New York City, they strike up a friendly conversation and shake hands on a partnership ("the only contract that ever existed between Cohan and Harris," Cohan wrote), agreeing to produce *Little Johnny Jones*. Based on the true-life background of the partnership, these scenes were close to Cohan's heart, and he lavished obvious care on the revised dialogue that he presented to Buckner for consideration.

The thematic elements that Buckner had worked so hard to expound in his draft of *Dandy* were not very flattering to Cohan. The song-and-dance man must have blanched at the "emotional blindness" that Warners had prescribed for his romance with Agnes, as well as the dismal failure of *Popularity*. Cohan felt that the drama of *Dandy* was implicit, that it was primarily an internal conflict between the character and his runaway ego. And since Cohan didn't have many failures in his life that he cared to recall, he certainly wasn't eager to have failures abound in a movie about his life. Taking issue, for instance, with a Buckner scene that illustrated the hardships of vaudeville life, Cohan suggested alternatively that Jerry and Nellie Cohan be comfortably retired by 1904 and that their struggle and deprivation be underplayed. Cohan added, "In direct contradiction of what is in the original script, I'm trying to show that the success of Cohan and his family has taken them out of the boarding house atmosphere entirely and with a good measure of the world's better things. Hence the summer home of the old folks and comfortable surroundings. I can see no value in further financial worries as I feel the earlier scenes have shown enough of that sort of thing and to me the story from now on is the problem of trying to mellow this young fellow and prevent him from building a lot of unnecessary obstacles in his path to future success." Ultimately, the Cohans do retire by 1904 in the completed *Dandy*. Likewise, George's love life in *Dandy* has none of Buckner's tragic coloration, and the flop of *Popularity* is handled with discretion. The schematic failures envisioned by Buckner in his early drafts were common-sensibly opposed by the Cagneys as well as Cohan eventually, and thus they are but a glimmer in the tapestry of the completed *Dandy*.

In many small ways, finally, Cohan bent over backward in his screenplay to portray himself in a sunny light, as a nice guy, as a nicer guy really than most contemporary accounts would allow. For example, Cohan purged all taunting remarks about his hometown of Providence from Buckner's drafts—a strange action, since Cohan, much like W. C. Fields and his "beloved" Philadelphia, cracked a lifetime of sarcastic jokes about his birthplace.[19] (Complaining about a Jerry Cohan line, "Who cares

19. Buckner, in lambasting Cohan's hometown of Providence, had merely done his homework well. Among the items in his clipping file of Cohan memorabilia was this stanza, for example, from Cohan's ditty "The Theatrical Situation, Alphabetically Speaking," which was written in balmier days, 1905: "In the twenty-six letters the Alphabet's got, / Not one stands for Providence, None in the lot; / I wouldn't insult the proud capital 'P.' / I can't stand for 'Prov,' / And it can't stand for me."

about Providence!", Cohan observed lamely, "That would of-
fend about four thousand friends of mine in that city.") The notorious Cohan ego (among the poems or essays he authored
during his career were "It's Great to be Great" and "Am I an
Egotist?") was offset by several patriotic speeches. And Cohan's
acrimonious feuding with critics was portrayed in Cohan's version as unfair, one-sided vendettas. In one awkwardly written
scene, the maligned George gives himself a peptalk about critics
in front of a mirror; in another, the sensitive song-and-dance
man is brought to tears by the vehemence and nastiness of
negative reviews.[20]

### Back to You, Bob

Buckner must have shuddered when confronted with the more
preposterous notions of Cohan's Screenplay, but he soldiered
on. His second Revised Screenplay (September 30, 1941) incorporated many of Cohan's suggested revisions (the final verdict
might be, *too many* of them). The opening White House scene,
for example, underwent revision. Some of Cohan's dialogue for
the scene was adopted "almost verbatim," in Buckner's words.
The "midnight conference" at the White House became "early
evening" at Cohan's request. "While still not literally true to
fact," according to notes inserted in the second Revised Screenplay for Cohan's benefit, "we hope this necessary compromise
is acceptable to you, for it gives us a much more dramatic opening. Also it is a more logical premise for assuming the use of the
President's time as he listens to the entire story; and it is

20. Cohan gives himself a peptalk in the mirror, in this excerpt from the
Buckner draft: "That's the way to talk to those babies, young fellow. Give them
something to write about. The false modesty stuff is no good. They won't print
it. Keep raving about yourself and telling them how wonderful you are. Never
mind what they say about you. Keep your name in print, that's the idea." Gore
Vidal has commented interestingly on "the obligatory mirror scene" that certain
writers feel compelled to interject into many books and movies in "The Top Ten
Best Sellers According to the Sunday *New York Times* as of January 7, 1973,"
*Matters of Fact and of Fiction: Essays, 1973–1976* (New York: Random House, 1978).

the only way we can effectively connect the beginning with the ending scenes. Thruout this prologue we have retained as many of your dialogue changes as space would allow." The matter of the "colored butler" was reconsidered yet affirmed, despite Cohan's objections. "We have checked your suggestion about the colored butler at the White House," the script noted, "and find that while either [Roosevelt aides] Mr. McIntyre or Mr. Cahill usually received callers, there was (and still is) a veteran colored butler who customarily escorted special visitors up to the President's study, especially when they arrived after dinner. This character's real value to the scene, however, is in further explaining your widespread reputation to the younger elements of the audience. This information is vital to the rest of the sequence."

The character of Agnes, meanwhile, became fictionalized as Mary for the first time and was integrated into the story earlier than before, in a vaudeville sequence in which she sings "Life's a Funny Proposition, after All," a Cohan tune. The relationship between her and George was still vague and platonic, but Cohan's plans for an elaborate romantic interlude in Europe in the final third of the story were scuttled. Warners (and Buckner) was firm about this, although the studio conceded other aspects of the still-negotiable relationship to Cohan. "By retaining the name 'Mary' for the girl we believe we are following your approval as stated in New York to Mr. Buckner," a script note explained. "It eliminates a too personal reference to actual persons, which may have disturbed you in certain scenes. Also, it gives a fine dramatic motivation to your composition of the great songs, 'Mary Is a Grand Old Name' and 'So Long, Mary' later in the picture. We are following your wish not to play any early love scenes. This is only a meeting, the beginning of a friendly theatrical relation, nothing more. But even platonically and casually, it is a great help to the story's construction to introduce Mary here, rather than in the last reel, as in your script."

Klaw and Erlanger's importance was minimized in this latest draft, in accord with Cohan's desires. Dietz and Goff made their

first, albeit dully written, appearances, as did Broadway inves-
tor Schwab (though he was called Swartz). It was Dietz and
Goff who provided a solution to the background of the Cohan-
Harris partnership. Cohan's proposed scene of Cohan and Harris meeting at a Staten Island baseball outing "would require
both too lengthy and elaborate production to justify a minor
story-point," according to the script notes, so Buckner created a
"short fictional scene to dramatize the start of the Cohan and
Harris partnership [that] is much shorter and more amusing"
than any in a previous draft. Cohan and Harris meet at the offices of Dietz and Goff after George has sung "Give My Regards
to Broadway" ("Harrigan" in the completed *Dandy*) to the un-
impressed duo. Harris too is peddling a script; all references to
"Terrible Terry" McGovern have been abandoned. This Buckner
scene has little of the comedy of the eventual scene in the Final
script—the best crack Dietz can muster is describing the Cohan
score as "epilepsy set to music"—but this "tight, integral link in
our construction," in Buckner's words, had nonetheless been
satisfactorily realized.[21]

Overall, Buckner still clung to the "knockdown" theory for

21. The breakup of the Cohan-Harris partnership, incidentally, was also a
scene that deeply concerned Cohan. Buckner's dialogue was all wrong in early
drafts, according to Cohan (who volunteered dialogue of his own in *his* draft of
the screenplay), and so was the chronology. The breakup had actually occurred
much earlier in Cohan's career than where Buckner had slotted it—and under
strained circumstances, as it turned out. Yet Buckner did not budge on this
score, clinging to his own fictionalized version of the breakup for dramatic purposes. "The fact that this breaking-up of the partnership actually took place
earlier than we indicate will, we hope, be excused here to help out continuity,"
read a note in the second Revised Screenplay. "It is of greater value at this point,
and except for a few professional show people with minor details, it should not
disturb anyone."

Among the "minor details" *Dandy* neglected to mention was the true motivation behind the Cohan-Harris split in 1919–20: Cohan's divisive activity during
the Actor's Equity strike. Although he was president of the Producing Manager's
Association, Harris "felt an instinctive sympathy for Equity which few of his
fellows shared," according to McCabe. Harris thought labor unions were an inevitable part of Broadway's future; Cohan hotly disagreed. On that discordant
note, very unlike the breakup as it is depicted in *Dandy*, the Cohan-Harris partnership was dissolved.

his screenplay and did not substantially revise the elements of tragedy and failure that characterized his early drafts. As Buckner explained in the script notes at one point (commenting on the drama of George's struggling during the vaudeville years):

It is vitally necessary to our dramatic construction that the success of you and your family *not* be assumed so conclusively this early in the picture. The struggles and problems of the boy are not those of the man. We lose all feeling of conflict and up-hill fighting if we now start moving merely from one successful play to another, as in your script. This point will be the first appearance of James Cagney, impersonating yourself, and it is extremely important that we build his character thru his reactions to trouble, if we are to get an audience to pull for him. It also wins sympathy for the family's struggle.

To accomplish this we have been forced to take a few liberties with the actual chronology of your early days on Broadway, when your almost uninterrupted success began with "The Governor's Son" and "Running for Office." Without this freedom of movement, while still being true to the general outline of your life, it is impossible for us to construct a tightly-knit personal story, which the motion-picture form requires. Therefore we will appreciate greatly your tolerant analysis of the following scenes as being less concerned with exact history than a carefully balanced series of dramatic elements which will play well.

Buckner and Warners likewise held sway on the crisis of *Popularity*, which was still deemed vital to the dramatic momentum of the script.[22] "It has an important human value to the story," Buckner argued in the script notes, "the comeback." The *Popularity* subplot was still overly complicated. Sam Forrest (a character who does not even appear in the completed *Dandy*) played a pivotal role; turn-of-the-century thespian Nat C. Goodwin cropped up as a character, precipitating the crisis by backing out of an agreement with Cohan to star in *Popularity*; and it was

22. The following speech by Sam Harris from Buckner's second Revised Screenplay is an example of this pumped-up theme of crisis: "We're staking a lot more than money, Forrest . . . George has never had a failure—not one in his whole life. And you never know, until a man gets knocked down, how well he can take a beating. George is the champ—the big fellow. He lives every bit of his publicity. He even *writes* most of it. That's what worries me—because I love the guy like a brother—and I'm afraid one good punch on the ego might fold him up—break his spirit and faith in himself."

Sam Harris who dictated the telegram of apology to the theater-going public (not George, as in the completed *Dandy*). Buckner did make some concessions to Cohan by "condensing and revising slightly" the angle of *Popularity*'s flop. For instance, the actual failure of the play was now dramatized by a rapid montage of hostile voices and melting marquee letters "blurring and running together in dismal defeat."[23] Diplomatically, Buckner argued that the minor revisions were sufficient. "In our original script, this incident's results were handled more freely and fictionally to emphasize your defeat in order to gain sympathy and understanding for a vital turning-point in your life. But since our version was too personal and historically inaccurate for your approval, we have, from necessity, deferred to your script, condensing and revising slightly, to keep up the speed of the story."

Again, it seemed that Cohan's most appreciated assistance was in the realm of music and musical staging. Cohan had complained about the use of "Is That Mr. O'Reilly?" as Jerry Cohan's novelty song, and Warners took him up on his offer to furnish "one of my father's own songs" (eventually, "The Dancing Master"). Cohan specifically requested a scene in which the Four Cohans could perform their famous "Goggles Doll House" routine, and Buckner complied in the second Revised Screenplay, noting, "Since this scene has been included at your special request, and we believe it will be a very entertaining bit for the family, could you furnish us with a brief description of the routine and its music?" (The "Goggles Doll House" routine was ultimately relegated to a montage snippet in the completed *Dandy*.)

Ironically, one particular song—a non-Cohan song—may have been the source of some unusual political pressure for Buckner at this stage. For if the storm clouds gathering over Europe impelled the makers of *Dandy* toward a national prepar-

23. The second Revised Screenplay added a "Note to Director: Any more detailed dramatization of the first-night failure of *Popularity* is open to discussion. It does not seem worthy of extensive footage to the writer. It was a dull play without music except for a background theme called 'The Popularity March,' which was later quite popular."

edness theme, they also created an atmosphere of political unity in Hollywood, as elsewhere in the land. Warner Brothers was anxious to prove itself patriotic and worried about offending FDR by the satire of *I'd Rather Be Right* (see figure 29). "The question of how much or how little of this show is to be included [in *Dandy*] is left open for decision," wrote Buckner in the script notes. "If, for some absurd reason, the great laughs in the lyrics of 'Off the Record' are thought censorable, the song can be eliminated and we could go straight into Cohan's dance routine."

## Enter, the Epsteins

Working against the clock, Buckner submitted the Temporary script (October 16, 1941) and its companion version, the Revised Temporary (October 30, 1941). Shooting was to begin in November. The chronology of Buckner's story line was now fairly well established, but, among other lingering deficiencies in the script, the romance between George and Mary was still not realized satisfactorily; Josie Cohan's part was still unduly small; George's own circle of cronies continued to have inflated roles; the flop of *Popularity* still carried unnecessary emphasis; and there was no deathbed scene for Jerry Cohan. Buckner's achievement in this, the last draft of the screenplay that he was actively involved in, consisted of synthesizing the disparate elements of Cohan's life and beginning to give them some dramatic shape. In addition, the lack of (acceptable) tragedy or theme in Cohan's life was beginning to emerge as a sort of common man subtext. The songs had been chosen and inserted by Buckner (and the Warners music department) at appropriate intervals in the story, even though the actual titles were juggled right up until shooting. These were achievements, yes. But the feeling of the Cagneys was that Buckner had deferred too much to Cohan in the writing and that in striving for the abstract demands of tragedy Buckner had missed the spirit of the great man's life.

There was even a worse problem from the Cagneys' point of view: Buckner, not a comedy writer, had written an unfunny script. With shooting only weeks away, the script "was sent to me [Cagney] at the Vineyard for approval. I read it with incredulity. There wasn't a single laugh in it, not the suggestion of a snicker. And this was a script purporting to be about a great American light entertainer, a professional humorist, a man who wrote forty-four Broadway shows, only two of which were not comedies. I said to brother Bill, 'It's no good. I won't touch it. But I tell you what I'll do. I'll give it a blanket O.K. now if you put the Epstein boys on it to liven it up and inject humor."[24]

The Epstein boys were Julius J. and Philip G. Epstein, identical twins with a reputation in Hollywood as witty and literate screenwriters who could doctor any ailing script. After coming to Hollywood from New York in the late thirties, they chalked up a number of prestige credits, including *Four Daughters* (1938), *The Man Who Came to Dinner* (1941), *The Male Animal* (1942), and *Arsenic and Old Lace* (1944). Though they were highly regarded for their stage and book adaptations, the Epsteins were awarded in 1943 their only Best Screenplay Oscar for an original that has since become a classic, *Casablanca* (a screenplay that Howard Koch also collaborated on, which has resulted in conflicting claims of authorship).[25] Philip G. Epstein died an untimely death in the early fifties, but Julius J. Epstein continued to work

24. Cagney, *Cagney by Cagney*, p. 105. In his letter to me, Buckner counters that Cagney "had agreed to play in the picture before the Epsteins were brought in for the jokes. This fact can be easily proved by studio records." Yet in his autobiography, Wallis would seem to support Cagney's memory, saying, "I was sadly disappointed when Cagney refused to make the picture. He said he was going into independent production and had absolutely no interest in Cohan. I asked Bill Cagney to put everything on hold. In record time, I had a skilled writer named Robert Buckner write a treatment and rushed it to Martha's Vineyard. No response. I called Bill again. He was lukewarm, but I got the impression I had made a dent in Jimmy's armor" (p. 103).
    One thing seems certain in any case: when the Buckner script was in the Cagneys' hands, Buckner stopped working on the project ("I did not work with the Epsteins at any time," says Buckner, "for no writers could be more unalike than ourselves"), the Epsteins came aboard, and at that point the "split" in the production team between Wallis-Buckner and the Cagneys began to tilt in favor of the Cagneys.
    25. For two books that offer Howard Koch's version of the writing of *Casablanca*, see his *Casablanca: Script and Legend* (New York: Overlook Press, 1973) and *As Time Goes By* (New York: Harcourt Brace Jovanovich, 1979). Note, however, that Julius J. Epstein has disputed Koch's memory regarding *Casablanca*.

regularly and is prospering into the eighties (his script for Howard Zieff's *House Calls* launched the recent TV series of the same name). The Cagneys had worked with the Epsteins often at Warners during the forties and trusted their professionalism. They were regarded as "two very bright lads" by James Cagney, who wrote, "They had invigorated the scripts of *Strawberry Blonde* and *The Bride Came C.O.D.*, and I knew and liked them both. The minute Phil and Julie went to work, I made the deal to do *Yankee Doodle Dandy*."[26]

The Epsteins didn't go to work right away, however. Associate producer William Cagney went to the Epstein brothers with a plea for their involvement. According to Julius J., "We never liked the subject, it was too sentimental for us. They [the Cagneys] asked us several times to do it, kept after us. We knew this fellow, Edmund Joseph, who had worked in vaudeville, writing skits. He needed the credit. We said, 'Why don't you put him on it? He comes from vaudeville, knows the background.'"[27] So William Cagney turned to Joseph, "a nice man who didn't have much of a career in Hollywood," according to Epstein. The Award-winning *Dandy* looks curious among Joseph's handful of screen credits, which include the undistinguished *Make Your Own Bed* (1944) and *Bowery to Broadway* (1944), as well as the Abbott-Costello features *Who Done It?* (1942) and *The Naughty Nineties* (1945). Of the four screenwriters who ultimately worked on *Dandy*, Joseph was the only one not under contract to Warners; he was brought in as a free-lancer from outside the gates. Although he did some tinkering with the script, sprinkled in a few jokes, and added some physical comedy, his contribution did not satisfy the Cagneys. "After he did a few things on it," says Epstein, "they still wanted us. The pressure grew. So we did it for Bill Cagney."[28]

26. Cagney, *Cagney by Cagney*, p. 105.
27. Interview with Julius J. Epstein, Boston, September 1979. An intriguing reference to another collaborator on the *Dandy* script, Joseph North, is made in 1974 program notes to a showing of *Dandy* in the Hal B. Wallis retrospective at the Los Angeles County Museum of Art. There is no evidence elsewhere of any screenwriting by a Joseph North, however, and it seems likely that it was an Edmund Joseph pseudonym at some stage in the project.
28. Interview with Epstein.

By now it was November, and shooting was due to begin on the musical numbers around Thanksgiving. Cagney was already in rehearsal for the dance routines and coming forward with a stream of ideas about how to reshape the script. It was a pressure-cooker situation, yet the Epsteins had always seemed to thrive in the pressure cooker (the story of the making of *Casablanca* is no less byzantine and pell-mell). With rehearsals in progress, the Epsteins began to examine the research and the various drafts, to take apart the screenplay and to put it back together again, a process that would continue right up until the end of filming with their rewriting pages daily on the set. It wasn't long before Buckner's Revised Temporary script was left behind; the Final script (November 25, 1941) of the Epsteins evidenced substantial rewriting in the dialogue and minor structural improvements. The dialogue transcript of the completed *Dandy* indicates another quantum rewrite, for not only the Epsteins but Cagney and to a lesser extent director Michael Curtiz rewrote dialogue and improvised bits of stage business while shooting *Dandy*.

The Epsteins' contribution pervades the script of *Dandy* as it was finally filmed, scene by scene, but they began their assignment by resolving one of the central nagging problems of the screenplay. First and foremost they had to contend with the character of Mary and with all the dead-end diversions that had been devised to keep her at arm's length from George during the history of the project. The Epsteins' solution was delightfully simple—they tossed out all the early drafts on her character and began anew. They wrote a scene in which the young George of vaudeville days is playing a bearded geezer on the stage in Buffalo (the inspiration came from Cohan's memory of playing "an old character actor, though I was a boy—I even played my own mother's father," recorded in the Cohan-Buckner interview transcript). After his performance, George is approached in his dressing room by a timid teen-ager named Mary (Joan Leslie) who is bursting with theatrical aspirations. "I'm eighteen—I sing and I dance and I'm going to New York, should I?" The bearded George impresses Mary with a springy buck-and-wing, his makeup is peeled away, and their sweet-natured (no "emotional blindness" in the Epsteins' version) romance is off to a whirling start. It's one of the most unabashedly charming scenes in the movie (see figure 5), and it sets the mood for the unadorned, old-fashioned romance that follows.

The Epsteins also expanded and revised the role of George's sister, Josie, in accordance with the Cagneys' wishes. Partly, Josie's role had shrunk during the evolution of the screenplay because she had actually left the Four Cohans over family tensions at one point and severed professional relations with the act. (Josie reportedly did not get along with Cohan's first wife; she and husband Fred Niblo, Jr., went into vaudeville together.) In the Epsteins' Final script, however, Josie's role was restored and spotlighted throughout *Dandy*. And there are *no* family tensions. When Josie quits the act to get married to "Fred," announcing her decision before Jerry Cohan's birthday party, George tells her warmly that she will be missed, that her departure is not, as Josie puts it, "just a simple case of subtraction" (see figure 21). This newly acquired focus on Josie made good dramatic sense, to be sure, but the Cagneys had an ulterior motive as well: Josie was to be played by their sister, Jeanne Cagney, a cum laude graduate of Hunter College who had worked her way up the ladder of the business through summer stock, radio drama, and "B" Hollywood pictures.[29]

Among other improvements in the Final script: the Epsteins

29. Jeanne Cagney's movie appearances include *All Women Have Secrets* (1939), *Golden Gloves* (1940), and *Queen of the Mob* (1940) before *Dandy*, and *The Time of Your Life* (1948), *Don't Bother to Knock* (1952), *Quicksand* (1950), *A Lion Is in the Streets* (1953), *Kentucky Rifle* (1955), *Man of a Thousand Faces* (1957), and *Town Tamer* (1965) afterwards.

Jeanne "had been the total student type [before being cast in *Dandy*], had never put one foot in front of the other athletically, and I knew that among other things, development of stamina was essential for her future in what is physically a very demanding business. She agreed, and I said, 'Get into a gymnasium, or better still, get to work with Johnny Boyle and have him teach you to dance for a solid six months. If you do that, moving from one place to another will never be a problem for you'. She said fine. That was June, and she started the dancing regimen in California with Johnny at once. I was in the East until November, and on my return what I saw absolutely stunned me. Jeannie was doing wings, cramp rolls, all kinds of buck dancing—really intricate steps, with full assurance and control. By the time *Yankee Doodle Dandy* came along, there was no doubt

threw out Cohan's circle of friends wholesale—Forrest, Dunn, and O'Brien, all unaccounted for in the completed *Dandy*. The Epsteins steered away from the alternating self-pity and self-congratulation of Buckner's approach. Scene by scene, they added jokes, colloquial dialogue, period references, bits that contributed to subtlety of character. The Dietz and Goff scene went through the typewriter again, producing the amusing Tweedledum and Tweedledee figures of the movie, both of them angels of Broadway who thrive on allowances from their wives. The brief but important scene (see figure 10) with Schwab was likewise infused with idiosyncratic humor (and the Epsteins—or Cagney—chose to switch the song that George sings in that scene to "Yankee Doodle Dandy," rather than the earlier, less rousing choice, "I Want to Be a Popular Millionaire"). They wrote a deathbed scene for Jerry Cohan that was heartrending. ("Curtiz kept saying, 'Give me the tear in the eye,'" according to Julius J. Epstein. "Finally, my brother said, 'Let's give him the tear in the eye.' So we wrote the death scene with the Cohan trademark—'My mother thanks you, my father thanks you,' and so on. We thought it was hilarious. We thought they'd never use it. But they did and it was one of the best scenes in the film.")[30] Buckner's powerful ending, with George tap-dancing down the White House stairs, was given an extra tug of emotion and immediacy by a coda written by the Epsteins showing George marching in step with a parade of soldiers who are singing "Over There" (see figure 32). The Epsteins, in this instance, were merely keeping up with the headlines. The Japanese had bombed Pearl Harbor on December 7, 1941. The Final script of *Dandy* had been approved by the studio two weeks earlier.

Nobody bothered to inform Cohan of these alterations in his life story, small or large, inconsequential or momentous. In fact, the revisions were made quietly and in. haste and were kept

---

she could play that lovely dancing lady, Josie Cohan, beautifully. It was, if I may say so, type casting" (Cagney, *Cagney by Cagney*, pp. 100–101).

30. Interview with Epstein.

from Cohan's knowledge. The Warners administration was feverish in its worry that the entire project was being jeopardized by the last-minute script surgery. But the Cagneys steamrolled on, benefactors of an unusual leverage with the studio higher-ups. After all, the Cagneys had dropped a bombshell of their own on the studio two weeks after the start of production: William Cagney informed studio head Jack Warner that brother James would not renew his contract with Warner Brothers after finishing *Dandy*. The studio tried every conceivable inducement to persuade James Cagney to reconsider. "As a result, William says, they were left alone to do exactly as they pleased with *Dandy*," according to the *New York Times* (January 10, 1943). "The Warners were 'prepared to make any concession.' They let William spend nearly $1,500,000 getting the picture exactly as he wanted it. James backed him up all the way."

## Just a Dancer Gone Wrong

Astaire had impeccable career judgment. That silky gentleman dancer would have been all wrong as the brash, cocky, irrepressible Cohan. But there was a logic in the casting of Cagney, just as there was a logic in the settling on Warner Brothers. Warners, after all, had carved a specialty niche for itself producing biographical pictures, or "biopics," as they were dubbed in the movie industry. During the thirties the studio had dramatized such great and famous lives as those of Louis Pasteur, Emile Zola, Disraeli, Elizabeth the Great, and footballer Knute Rockne. The studio had made a name for itself producing backstage musicals also, pictures like *42nd Street* (1933) and (with Cagney in the cast) *Footlight Parade* (1933). Cagney always liked to describe himself as, at heart, a song-and-dance man who was led down the wayward path of gangsterism by the movies. "Just a dancer gone wrong," was how pal and frequent co-star Pat O'Brien described Cagney,[31] and that may be his most fitting epitaph. Just as the virulent social consciousness of Warner

31. Pat O'Brien, *The Wind at My Back* (Garden City, N.Y.: Doubleday, 1964), p. 128.

Brothers in the thirties found its expression in the Cagney persona, so too would the studio's tide of patriotism in the forties find its symbol in James Cagney.[32]

In 1941, as Cohan was dying, Cagney was peaking in popularity. He was at a turning point in his career. At forty-two he was the top box-office attraction at Warner Brothers among the male stars (Bogart had not yet hit his stride). Cagney was restless, enigmatic, a man of private contradictions. He had epitomized the motion picture "tough guy" since his explosive performance as Depression era rumrunner Tom Powers in William Wellman's *The Public Enemy* (1931). Yet he was an amateur artist, a poet, a conservationist, and he led a quiet home life with his wife. In the thirties, Cagney was a left-liberal activist, an organizer of the Screen Actors Guild (later, its president), a zealous supporter of FDR, a contributor to a multitude of social causes. With Warners and *Dandy* and the post-World War II wave of anticommunism, his politics drifted to the right. Late in life, he would enthusiastically support Ronald Reagan for president and describe himself as an "arch-conservative." This Cagney of shifting temperament had never been very content with his one-dimensional tough guy image, and during the thirties he executed a highly publicized series of walkouts and contractual lawsuits against Warner Brothers in an effort to redress his working conditions and end his typecasting. By the advent of *Dandy*, he was chafing at the bit to do a full-blown musical. "Psychologically, I needed no preparation for *Yankee Doodle Dandy*, or professionally either," wrote Cagney. "I didn't have to pretend to be a song-and-dance man. I was one."[33]

Unfortunately, Cagney enacted few song-and-dance roles in his long career. Besides *Dandy* there is the prototypical backstage musical *Footlight Parade* (1933); a low-budget lark, *Something to Sing About* (1937), produced for a fly-by-night independent company during one of Cagney's walkouts; the disappointing *West Point Story* (1950); and a tuneful parable

---

32. See Andrew Bergman's sociological film survey, *We're in the Money: Depression America and Its Films* (New York: Harper and Colophon, 1972).

33. Cagney, *Cagney by Cagney*, p. 103.

about corrupt unions, *Never Steal Anything Small* (1958). Yet the actor whose name evokes a slew of memorable tough guy characterizations in movies was an ardent dance buff during his entire lifetime. He actually entered the profession as a dancer, playing a "female impersonator" in the chorus line of Phil Dunning's *Every Sailor* revue in 1919. Then he joined the vaudeville circuit as a song-and-dance man, graduating to "legit" plays on Broadway while also staging dances for popular musical revues of the period. To make ends meet, he ran the Cagné School of Dance in New Jersey for a spell. Later, when he came to Hollywood, Cagney took ballet lessons from the famous Kosloff, from Billy Droyer, and from Eduardo Cansino (the last a well-known Spanish dancer who was the father of Rita Hayworth). Half a century later, there was really nothing eyebrow-raising about the item reported in the Hollywood trade papers one day: After years of retirement and seclusion, the aging Cagney had been spotted down at the old Gower Gulch studios one afternoon, swapping jazz tap dance steps with classical ballet star Mikhail Baryshnikov.

For two months before the actual filming of *Dandy*, according to publicity for the film, Cagney rehearsed the dance sequences. He and his sister Jeanne practiced for four hours daily and then, during shooting, from seven to nine in the morning and for two hours every night after "wrap." Cagney's instructor was Johnny Boyle, known to aficionados as "the dancer's dancer." Boyle had been featured on Broadway in Cohan-Harris revues and had staged dances for Cohan from 1906 to 1922. More recently, he had been working in Hollywood as a choreographer and specialty dancer for motion pictures. Boyle can be spotted in the chorus of Cagney's *Something to Sing About*, and it is possible that he was somehow involved in the production of Cohan's *The Phantom President* as well. Both of these movies have moments of choreography that are uncannily similar to highlights of *Dandy*. There is a scene in *The Phantom President*, for example, in which Cohan, performing in blackface, sings a tune entitled "Maybe Someone Ought to Wave the Flag," then does a tap dance on the apron stage of his minstrel show that was copied later, nearly step for step, for Cagney's "Yankee Doodle Dandy" number in *Dandy* (Cohan, like Cagney in *Dandy*, even dances up the side of a wall—see figure 11). There is a scene in *Something to Sing About* with Cagney, as George was to do in the finale of *Dandy* (see figure 31), tap-dancing merrily down a long flight of steps. Boyle knew Cohan's dancing style, his "stiff-legged technique and his run up the side of the proscenium arch."[34] Boyle showed Cagney Cohan's mannerisms and "he showed me all the things Cohan did on stage."[35] The rehearsals for *Dandy* were so strenuous that, at one point, Boyle hurt "one foot badly enough to be virtually incapacitated for dancing the rest of his life."[36]

Characteristically, with all this preparation and rehearsal, Cagney still didn't feel quite ready when he went before the cameras. Workhorse and disciplined professional that he was, Cagney fretted that his dancing was not on a par with Cohan's. The first production number to be filmed was "I Was Born in Virginia" (glimpsed in the montage sequences—see figure 6), and Cagney the perfectionist "went onto the shooting stage not knowing entirely what I was going to do. It got by, but I didn't feel right about it." Then Curtiz shot the memorable "Yankee Doodle Dandy" number from the play *Little Johnny Jones*, a spectacular highpoint of *Dandy* (see figures 11–13). Again, Cagney didn't measure up to his own high standards. "Again not enough rehearsal and again apparently nobody noticed it, but I did. There was a rigidity in certain areas of the number because I wasn't always sure of what the next step was going to be."[37]

The challenges were different for evoking Cohan in the nonmusical sequences of *Dandy*. Cagney was an expert mimic; he could easily imitate individual quirks, dialects, accents, physical gestures. Cagney had only met Cohan once, in 1926, when Cohan was casting one of his plays. "I was in and out in a great hurry," Cagney recalls, "Cohan holding I was not the type he was looking for."[38] Cagney had also attended Cohan's stage per-

34. Cagney, *Cagney by Cagney*, p. 105.
35. "James Cagney Talking," *Films and Filming*, March 1959.
36. Cagney, *Cagney by Cagney*, p. 105.
37. Cagney, *Cagney by Cagney*, p. 105.
38. Cagney to McGilligan, July 3, 1979.

formance in *Ah, Wilderness!* in 1934 and possibly (accounts vary) *I'd Rather Be Right.* Cohan's acting in *Ah, Wilderness!* was "simply marvelous," Cagney recalls. "It was truly a great performance. His mannerisms, which were a holdover from earlier times, were not in evidence when he was doing that job." Cagney screened *The Phantom President* in preparation for *Dandy* as well, but "it was a flop, and Mr. Cohan's mannered performance did not help it any."[39] Regardless, Cagney's sharp memory and diligent research provided him with an arsenal of those mannerisms: Cohan's peculiar stride, his way of nodding and winking to evidence approval, his New England drawl, his leading with his chin, his monkeylike stance.

The only question was how fully Cagney should deploy those mannerisms. Typically, the actor consulted with a group of his peers with whom he used to have a dinner get-together every Tuesday night, asking their advice about the role he was to play. "When it was announced that I was to play Cohan, I told the boys what my plans for him were," Cagney recalls. "I did play him as straight as I could, in the off stage sequences, and used his mannerisms only when the opportunities presented themselves, without dragging them in unnecessarily. Apparently that worked, because they all agreed that was the sensible approach."[40]

39. Cagney to McGilligan, July 3, 1979.

40. Cagney to McGilligan, July 3, 1979. See also, "James Cagney Talking," *Films and Filming*: "What most people don't know is that Cohan was a very flamboyant man. Whether off-stage or on, he was always full of gestures. So, one night, I had a dinner party with a lot of friends of mine who had worked with Cohan. Among them Spencer Tracy (who had worked in a show that had been directed by Cohan); Lynn Overman, a fine character actor; Frank McHugh; Ralph Bellamy knew him, Frank Morgan was at the gathering . . .

"So I said, 'Boys, I've got a problem here, and I want to throw it over to you. You all know Cohan much better than I, and I want your opinions. I think it might be a good idea not to try to be Cohan off-stage. To do all the Cohanesque mannerisms on-stage and on-stage only; and then to try to play it as straight as I can off-stage.'

"They thought it was a good idea, and I did it that way. The reasons being that as soon as the trick is over-emphasized, the impersonation becomes too important and there's no performance, it gets in the way."

## Mike Curtiz and Company

The remaining members of the *Dandy* cast were, by and large, Warner Brothers contract players. Besides Cagney as George M., the Cohan family was portrayed by Cagney's sister Jeanne as Josie, radio actress Rosemary DeCamp as Nellie Cohan, and Walter Huston, father of writer-director John Huston, a durable ex-vaudevillian who had played everything from Lincoln to *Dodsworth* in the movies, in a delightful change of pace as Jerry Cohan. Youthful (she celebrated her seventeenth birthday during shooting of *Dandy*), Detroit-born Joan Leslie played Mary as all sweetness and light; it was the second movie in a career that never fulfilled its early glow. (Leslie had made her debut as Gary Cooper's costar in *Sergeant York* in 1941.) Richard Whorf from Broadway, an ex-classical actor who had performed with the Alfred Lunt–Lynn Fontanne troupe, played Cohan's partner, Sam Harris. Radio and stage songstress Irene Manning (known to radio audiences as Hope Manning) played soubrette Fay Templeton (see figure 17). Veteran character actor and master of accents George Tobias played stage producer Dietz. Eddie Foy had an extended cameo playing his own father, Eddie Foy, Sr. The familiar faces with bits or walk-ons included S. Z. Sakall (Schwab), Walter Catlett (vaudeville manager), and Captain Jack Young (seen only from the back) as the magisterial voice of the president.

The director was one of the lot's finest, Michael Curtiz. Curtiz, like Buckner, was not a logical choice on the evidence of his credentials, despite his studio loyalties—his forte was not really musicals. Curtiz could pull almost any rabbit out of his hat, however. Once an actor and producer in the Budapest theater, the Hungarian-born Mihaly Kertesz had worked in the cinema in Sweden and Hungary, served in World War I, and directed films in Germany before being lured to Hollywood by Harry Warner in 1926. His career is something of a mystery today. In the abundance of film books on the market, there is as yet not one entirely devoted to Curtiz's rich lifetime of work. Yet he was arguably Warner Brothers' most versatile, prolific, and consistently enjoyable craftsman, with credits at the studio from 1927 to 1953. His work in the thirties includes the Errol Flynn swashbucklers *Captain Blood* (1935), *The Adventures of Robin Hood* (codirected with William Keighley, 1938), and *The Sea Hawk* (1940), as well as two very different Cagney outings, the screwball comedy *Jimmy the Gent* (1935) and the gangster melodrama *Angels with Dirty Faces* in 1938. (In 1942, Curtiz directed Cagney's first Technicolor feature, *Captains of the Clouds*.) The forties was Curtiz's golden period at Warners, marked by the "unrivalled trinity," in David Thomson's phrase, of *Yankee Doodle Dandy* (1942), *Casablanca* (1943), and *Mildred Pierce* (1945), the "most enjoyable of biopics," the "best of wartime espionage" and "the most throbbing of Joan Crawford melodramas."[41] Vehicles for Cagney, Bogart, and Joan Crawford, respectively, under Curtiz's direction these three pictures became more than just showcases; they became classics, expressive and enduring works that feature three of Warners' most vital, popular, iconic stars.

Whatever else he was, Curtiz was a director who could make the trains run on time. Known as Iron Mike for his martinet attitude, Curtiz is the subject of countless anecdotes in Hollywood lore for his mangling of the English language. (One example: "Smile with the coat buttoned.") He was said to have trouble with the vernacular of his screenplays (his second wife, screenwriter Bess Meredyth, reportedly helped him decipher his scripts). But it seems that he had a facility for dealing with the studio bureaucracy and the necessary speed of a studio timetable. He had a habit of surrounding himself with the most talented people on the Warner Brothers lot. And mangled English aside, it seems that he had an intuitive grasp of cinema, an acknowledged *noir* sensibility as well as a blistering comic impulse, a knack for pacing, "letting air in at certain spots to prevent it [any movie] from being unadulterated rush."[42] Curtiz

41. See entry under Curtiz in David Thomson's *A Biographical Dictionary of Film* (New York: William Morrow, 1976).
42. Cagney, *Cagney by Cagney*, p. 172.

was helpful to his actors too, although it may have been inadvertent to some extent. In his memoirs, Cagney tells an amusing anecdote about Curtiz's demonstrating a scene (probably for *Jimmy the Gent*) "with all the old fancy European techniques— brushing off the cuffs with a flick of the finger, reaching fussily for a cigarette and lighting it with a flourish, then putting his foot on a bench, and proceeding to talk with one hand on the hip."[43] Cagney mimicked the director perfectly, carrying it to the point of absurdity, until Curtiz surrendered. Then Cagney performed the scene the only way he knew how, his way. "Curtiz . . . wore his coat of many colors rather well, and he was most unhappy when off the set," Cagney recalls. "I used to say there was no such person as Curtiz, but only Curtiz the director. I understand they would actually take the camera from him to keep him from going on for 24 hours of straight shooting. He was truly fanatical. I understand he had no life off the set."[44]

The other contributions to *Dandy* are of interest. The choreography credit eventually read: "James Cagney's Dances Routined by John Boyle." The technical adviser for the picture was William Collier, Sr., a former Weber and Fields farceur who had appeared in Cohan revues, had been compared in his performance style to Cohan, and maintained a friendship with Cohan that lasted until his death. The makeup was by Perc Westmore of the Westmore family, a dynasty long associated with Warner Brothers. The costumes were designed by Milo Anderson. The montage sequences were assembled by Don Siegel, early in his

43. Cagney, *Cagney by Cagney*, p. 150.

44. Cagney to McGilligan, August 27, 1979.

Buckner adds this note about Curtiz's relationship to the script. "Curtiz did not work personally on the screenplay. I made six or seven films with Mike and never had any trouble with him this way. Only occasionally, when his wife Bess Meredith [sic], an old silent-film writer of some fame, would do a little homework (unasked) on the scripts. Unasked by the writers, I mean. Mike undoubtedly asked her, as he never understood English very well and suffered severely with the Hungarian Disease of duplicity. I don't think Bess had any hand in *Yankee Doodle Dandy*, but who can ever be sure about pillow talk?" (Buckner to McGilligan, August 7, 1980).

Also, see Wallis and Higham's *Star Maker* for some intriguing material about Curtiz's incorrigible habit of tinkering with his scripts, one way or another.

career, before his reputation blossomed as an action director. The art director (the studio had to build 285 separate sets for *Dandy*, according to studio publicity) was Carl Jules Weyl, an ex-architect from Stuttgart, Germany, who won an Oscar for *The Adventures of Robin Hood* and then amassed an impressive string of studio credits, including *The Letter* (1940), *King's Row* (1941), and *The Big Sleep* (1946), before dying of leukemia in 1948. The director of cinematography was James Wong Howe, born in Canton, China, a reportedly cantankerous veteran who began a long career noted for its naturalistic excellence in the silent era under showman Cecil B. DeMille.[45]

The musical scoring and staging of *Dandy* was the studio's proudest achievement. The representative arrangement of Cohan's vast musical output posed a challenge well met by the Warner music and dance departments, not only by the choral fireworks of such extravaganzas as "You're a Grand Old Flag," but such deceptively and simply staged numbers as "Mary" or "Harrigan." Stalwart Leo F. Forbstein was musical director, orchestral arrangements were by Ray Heindorf.[46] Forbstein was an ex-fiddle player with Grauman's Chinese Theater in Hollywood and ran the music department at Warners during the studio's halcyon days, nourishing such notables as songwriters Harry Warren and Al Dubin, symphonic composer Erich Wolf-

45. The sometimes quarrelsome Wong Howe, one of the great cinematographers in Hollywood history, discounted his work on *Dandy* in his twilight years and had very little to say that was positive about either the photographic style or director Curtiz. According to Wong Howe's recollections in Charles Higham's *Hollywood Cameramen* (Bloomington: Indiana University Press, 1970): "*Yankee Doodle Dandy* . . . had very few photographic opportunities; I had to create them. Mike Curtiz knew almost nothing about lighting; he couldn't even tell the cameraman how he wanted the lights to look. He was very dominating, and many of his ideas wouldn't work. The dances were done by Busby Berkeley, and I enjoyed doing those more, but generally it was an uninteresting picture cinematically" (p. 88). Wong Howe's memory appears to be faulty about Berkeley's contribution to the musical staging of *Dandy* (since there is little evidence elsewhere to suggest that Berkeley was at all involved). Berkeley may have had some input, but it was probably marginal.

46. For further information about Warner Brothers' talented music department, see James R. Silke's *Here's Looking at You, Kid: 50 Years of Fighting, Working and Dreaming at Warner Bros.* (Boston: Little, Brown, 1976).

gang Korngold, composer-arranger Heinz Roemheld (drafted for work on *Dandy*), and composer-conductor Max Steiner. Heindorf, a piano player at the Coconut Grove before joining the studio, actually did much of the work for Forbstein, choosing the musicians, tracking the music, and often wielding the baton. The production numbers (which strove, whenever possible, to be replicas of the Cohan originals) were to the shared credit of Seymour Felix and LeRoy Prinz. Felix was an ex-dance director of many Florenz Ziegfeld musicals and had won a special Oscar for the dance number "A Pretty Girl Is like a Melody" from *The Great Ziegfeld* in 1936. Prinz, a Missouri-born choreographer, had directed dance in Europe for Max Reinhardt and choreographed for the Folies Bergère.

There is a curious footnote to the story of the writing of the screenplay. Although the tentative credits for *Dandy* were listed by the studio as original story by Robert Buckner, screenplay by Buckner, Edmund Joseph, Julius J. and Philip G. Epstein (to which the *Variety* review of May 29, 1942, added, "Based on a story of George M. Cohan"), the Epsteins were absented from the credits on the screen. "In those days, the credits had no financial meaning," Julius J. Epstein explains, "so we stepped aside for Buckner and Joseph. Besides, we really didn't consider it to be one of our scripts."[47] Buckner says he did not think the Epsteins deserved co-credit, and fought that possibility with a threat of going to arbitration. Thus, screenplay credit went to Buckner and Joseph, story credit to Buckner, with no mention of the Epsteins and no mention of Cohan except above the title. The Cagneys added their own parenthetical note, however, by taking out a full-page advertisement in the Hollywood trade papers shortly after the release of *Dandy*, publicly thanking the Epstein brothers for their valuable contribution to the screenplay. "Although we were grateful, it was embarrassing to us," Julius J. Epstein recalls, "and it was demeaning to Joseph and Buckner."[48]

47. Interview with Epstein.
48. Interview with Epstein.

## Yankee Doodle Success

Shooting was completed in early 1942. The Epsteins, the Cagneys, and Curtiz had continued to add bits, dialogue changes, colloquial speech, and comic touches right up until the last minute before shooting (and *during* shooting as well). Nearly every scene underwent some modest surgery; dialogue was condensed or tightened, transitions were smoothed, the jokes were smartened up, and the relationships were enhanced. The structure of the story necessarily fell into its final sequence. The order of Fay Templeton's songs was reversed, for example; a scene with the Cohan family stranded in a Midwest railroad waiting room was switched in the plot's chronology with a scene in which George encounters Eddie Foy outside a Broadway theater. (The Foy scene is an example of a scene that didn't even make it into the Final script, although a shorter version of it appears in an earlier Buckner draft.) At least one scene—a brief, transitional one with the Cohan youngsters, Josie and George—was cut entirely from the picture. And, importantly, virtually all of the *Dandy* narration underwent extensive rewriting, probably during postproduction, to complement the editing process. In its final form, this narration is characterized by a heightened historic and nostalgic flavor, and it provides the apt thread of narrative continuity. The Epsteins apparently stayed around long enough to write this revised narration, but Cagney's hand in the phraseology seems evident also.

For that matter, Cagney's hand seems evident throughout. That crucial first scene between George and Mary, for example, was given another once-over after the Final script was approved. Cagney's funny clicking noise with his mouth, the invitation to go out for a "cold bottle and a bird," the business at the end of the scene when George stomps on his beard—these are among the touches unaccounted for in the Final script and probably contributed by Cagney. Likewise, the scene between George and Eddie Foy (see figure 18), with Cagney imitating Foy's lisp and habit of talking with one hand cupped over his mouth, runs on in *Dandy* as if it were partly improvised. Among the other unmistakable Cagney touches were his tears at Jerry

Cohan's bedside (see figure 25), an icing-on-the-cake not written into the Final.[49]

Of his participation in the script itself, Cagney has said only, "There were many things which I dropped into the script. But that was true of all our jobs for some of us."[50] In interviews he has characteristically given full credit to others—to his brother and to the Epsteins, in particular, undercutting Buckner. Yet it seems that his own involvement was in many ways the creative force that guided the screenplay to its ultimate reckoning. The surprise is that, for a script with such a layered history, *Dandy* actually held together wonderfully well on the screen, better than in any one of the previous drafts, better even than in the Final script. "I can understand the mystery involved in the final script of *Yankee Doodle Dandy*," Cagney acknowledges. "The Epstein boys were responsible for most of the re-write. There is no reason for you to know that, or [that] through the shooting scripts *there were interpolations by actors and directors concerned with it.* [Emphasis added.] Curtiz did have very little to do with that, as his knowledge of English was very spare. Joseph was a writer who, as I understand it, and I never met him, needed the credit, and the Epstein boys put his name in in place of their own as a favor to a friend. Buckner, who decidedly lacked any imagination, as far as I could find out, contributed little and I withheld approval of the script until the Epstein boys were put on it. They were bright and charming young men, and very likeable."[51]

49. Writing about the pleasure of working with old pro Walter Huston, Cagney referred to the deathbed scene in his autobiography: "I knew we were working well together when after we finished Walter's death scene in which I collapse weeping in his arms, I turned to hard-boiled Mike Curtiz and saw tears streaming down his cheeks. 'Cheeses Chrisdt, Jimmy,' he said, 'beautiful, beautiful.' That may have been the ultimate compliment" (Cagney, *Cagney by Cagney*, p. 106). Cagney adds, "The crying . . . just seemed to do the finishing off of what was in the script" (Cagney to McGilligan, August 27, 1979).

50. Cagney to McGilligan, August 27, 1979.

51. Cagney to McGilligan, August 27, 1979.

As indicated elsewhere, Buckner hotly disputes Cagney's recollection of events surrounding the writing of *Dandy*, as well as his value judgements. Buckner says: "These many versions of the script are always a sore point with the writers concerned on a film. That I wrote the treatment or format that was

At slightly over two hours, the final cut of *Dandy* was rather long, and thus some minor scenes (some vaudeville scenes illustrating George's upward climb) were left on the cutting-room floor.[52] Advance word in Hollywood was high. Warner Brothers cranked up its promotion unit to ensure what many studio insiders felt was going to be a smash hit, regardless. The premiere of *Dandy* was set for July 4, 1942, Cohan's birthday. Then, Cohan had an operation in January "which revealed that his cancer had spread devastatingly. He was aware that a virtual death sentence had been passed on him, but his bravery was unwa-

---

used, and the first draft, and subsequent contributions, no one can truthfully deny. Otherwise how would I have received the solo credit for the Original Story and first credit for the screenplay? Our Screen Writer's Guild would never have permitted it otherwise. There had to be several versions of the script before Cohan was completely satisfied with every line and scene. The Epstein brothers were brought into the picture later on as jokesmiths and gag writers but they made no structural contributions of note to the final film. As for Edmund Joseph, no one can quite remember him. He was brought in by his friends the Epsteins for a free ride on the credits. When I contested the Epsteins being credited on the screenplay they withdrew any claim, but instead slipped in Joseph somehow. The Epsteins were talented gag-men and Curtiz, the director, was one of their aficionados."

In regard to the Epsteins, Buckner adds, "If their contribution was in any way a major one so would their credits have been on the screen. They were never noted for their shyness about claiming credit. . . . If you can believe that the Epsteins 'didn't care to be included' in the screen credits (the only measure by which film writers live and progress, financially and reputation-wise), you must also believe in fairies."

As for Cagney's contributions to the script, Buckner says, "That Cagney added some gags and bits of his own I am certain is right. He was always very good at this in all of his pictures, and all his writers were grateful for it, including me. . . . I don't know precisely what touches Cagney added to the script, but they were several and valuable I have no doubt. Certainly no actor in Hollywood history ever had a role so beautifully tailored to his own personality, physical appearance or talents. Not even Gable in *Gone with the Wind* or George Arliss in *Disraeli*. That it gave him his Oscar was a just reward" (Buckner to McGilligan, August 7, 1980).

52. Cut from final print—Actors: Vera Lewis, Jim Toney, Charles Drake; Receptionist: Ann Doran; Porter: Napoleon Simpson; Call Boy: Buddy (Lon) McCallister; Housekeeper: Leah Baird. Source: Homer Dickens, *The Films of James Cagney* (Secaucus, N.J.: Citadel Press, 1972).

vering."[53] In deference to Cohan, Warners moved up the official release date.

The world premiere of *Yankee Doodle Dandy* was held on May 29, 1942, as a war bonds benefit. Top balcony seats cost $25, loges went for $25,000. Alfred E. Smith was there, as was Al Jolson; Governor Herbert H. Lehman of New York and Mayor Fiorello H. LaGuardia presented citations. The gala raised $4,750,000 in war bonds. The Warners publicity department tied in with women's clubs and defense plants; sheet music, RCA Victor record albums (three records, six sides—$2.10), cosmetics from the Warners-affiliated House of Westmore in New York, *Yankee Doodle Dandy* ties, even evening gowns (modeled in advertisements by Joan Leslie, "in the flag blue or red combined with the frothy white net and dazzling white faille bolero"). Exhibitors were serviced with *Dandy* front displays, overheads, lobby cutouts, instructions for holding Cohan impressionists contests, and local talent hunts for brother-sister acts. *Parents' Magazine*, with a readership of two million parents and teachers, selected *Dandy* picture of the month.

Yet it may be that no picture ever needed such a gala launching less or so aptly caught the prevailing mood of the nation in its star-spangled patriotism. There is a tendency among latter-day critics to sneer at the well-crafted formula of *Dandy*. After all, the movie broke no new ground cinematically and really had little influence on the subsequent evolution of the movie musical, other than by its example as a successful "biopic." Critic Andrew Sarris has lamented its "frenzied flag-waving and family sentimentality."[54] Even so professed an admirer of the picture as Andrew Bergman has qualified his praise by describing *Dandy* as a "solid movie musical, if a definitely old-fashioned bit of show biz hokum."[55] But that is the reaction nowadays, and scarcely unanimous at that. Then, it was nearly impossible not to be swept away by *Dandy's* locomotive pace,

53. McCabe, *George M. Cohan*, p. 265.

54. Sarris is quoted from the Introduction to the Da Capo edition of *Cagney: The Actor as Auteur* by Patrick McGilligan (New York, 1980).

55. Andrew Bergman, *James Cagney* (New York: Pyramid, 1973), p. 98.

by the onrush of dramatized history, by the nostalgic depiction of vaudeville, by the thinly veiled call to unity and prepared-ness, by the foot-tapping musicality of the piece, by the profes-sionalism of the company, above all by the Cohan of Cagney. If Buckner and associates had not quite managed to produce a masterful screenplay, if the script for *Dandy* fell short on char-acter, insight, resonant theme, and the factual contours of Co-han's life—somehow that didn't matter. The movie that emerged instead was a Horatio Algerish fantasy based on that life, and very much in the spirit of the hour.

However he managed to do it, Curtiz did his job as director remarkably well. Usually jaundiced and cynical in his vision, here the Hungarian-born Curtiz wore the love of his adopted country proudly on his sleeve. *Dandy* was a very personal film for Curtiz too, and one that marshaled all of his feeling and tricks. The knockabout pacing, the cheap sentimentality, the rough comedy—these were all Curtiz specialties. And though the seamless camerawork of *Dandy* is often overshadowed by the performances of the stars, the movie's visual style was char-acteristic of Curtiz in its control and momentum: the tense com-positions in such emotional scenes as Jerry Cohan's death (see figure 25); the elaborate, deep-focus, point-of-view shots that would be conspicuous elsewhere but are taken for granted in *Dandy*'s tightly exploding *mise-en-scène* (see figures 8 and 17); the beautifully staged and photographed musical numbers that are intercut in perspective between chorus groupings and intimate star turns. Unsurprisingly (but nonetheless, effectively), the re-sult of Curtiz's visual strategy was to favor George at all points in the story, thereby consolidating the movie around Cagney's tour de force characterization.

Foremost, *Dandy* was Cagney's triumph. In George, Cagney had found the role he would want to be remembered for. With *White Heat* (the two movies that bookended Cagney's career in the forties could not have been more unalike), it is one of his two most sublime and captivating performances. He completely inhabited the part, got under Cohan's skin. "He caught more than a touch of Cohan's self-love," wrote Bergman, "but managed to make the character a good deal more sympathetic than Cohan was in actuality."[56] The movie validated Cagney for all time as a song-and-dance man; the boundless and explosive dancer, the clipped and heartfelt singer, the light and bantering comedian—they were the alter ego of the tough guy that movie audiences had grown accustomed to. That is why *Dandy* is Cagney's favorite picture, the one most congenial to himself. In a way, *Dandy* was autobiographical for Cagney because he had so much in common with its subject, George M. Cohan—the vaudeville years, the rags to riches career, the furious patriotism, the reclusive retirement. Or as Cagney liked to put it, simply, once a song-and-dance man, *always* a song-and-dance man.

The critics of the era had almost nothing but accolades for *Dandy*. *Variety* wrote, "This spellbinding drama will establish itself firmly among the superlative pictures of all times." Archer Winston of the *New York Post* wrote, "*Yankee Doodle Dandy* . . . is as perfectly timed for 1942 as *Sergeant York* was for 1941. The latter came to a nation moving reluctantly into war, matched its objections with a famous conscientious objector of the last war, and solved his and our problems in a magnificent real life display of heroism. The former . . . comes as our soldiers and sailors depart to fight on the seven seas and five continents. What could be more timely than to have recalled for us the career of America's lustiest flag-waver, the author of 'Over There'?" Wrote Howard Barnes of the *New York Herald Tribune*, "The magic of *Yankee Doodle Dandy* is conjured up by the consummate Cagney portrayal. He even looks like Cohan at times and he has the great man's routines down cold. The point is that he adds his own individual reflections to the part, as should certainly be done in any dramatic impersonation of a celebrated figure. He has given many memorable and varied screen performances in the past, but this is nothing short of a brilliant tour-de-force of make-believe."

Cagney garnered his second New York Film Critics prize for Best Acting for *Dandy* (the first was in 1939 for *Angels with Dirty Faces*). The movie was also nominated for eight Academy

56. Bergman, *James Cagney*, p. 92.

Awards: Best Picture, Best Supporting Actor (Huston), Original Story (Buckner), Director (Curtiz), Editing (George Amy), Sound (Nathan Levinson), Musical Scoring (Heinz Roemheld and Ray Heindorf), and Actor (Cagney).[57] The war was uppermost in the Academy's mind that year. Marine Private Tyrone Power and Air Force Private Alan Ladd unfurled service flags at the Oscar ceremonies disclosing 27,677 names of industry people in uniform. Messages were read from Madame Chiang Kai-shek and FDR. Jeannette MacDonald sang the national anthem. The usually bronze-filled, gold-plated Oscar statue was cast in plaster for wartime reasons. It would seem that the patriotic *Dandy* had an edge, yet MGM's *Mrs. Miniver* prevailed in the awards, and the only *Dandy* winners were Levinson, Roemheld and Heindorf, and Cagney. Greer Garson's acceptance speech as Best Actress rambled over an hour. The Oscar ceremonies "reached a new high in sappiness that night," according to one contemporary account, "which was partly redeemed by Cagney's simple gesture."[58] When Gary Cooper tore open the Best Actor envelope and announced the winner, Cagney stepped to the podium without fanfare. "I've always maintained," he told the glittering Hollywood crowd, "that in this business you are only as good as the other fellow thinks you are. It's nice to know that you people thought I did a good job. And don't forget that it was a good part, too. Thank you very much." The next morning, it is said, Cagney walked into his brother's office and put the Oscar on William Cagney's desk as a private gesture of appreciation.

57. Amy was a veteran film editor. Colonel Nathan Levinson was head of the Warners sound department and a pioneer in the development of talking pictures. Heinz Roemheld was one of the arranger-composers in the Warners stable, best known for his musical adaptation of Sigmund Romberg's operetta, *The Desert Song*, the third motion picture version, in 1953. Curiously, Roemheld's name doesn't even show up on the film credits, although the Oscar went to him and Heindorf jointly. In his letter to me Buckner says flatly, "I have no recollection of this Heinz Roemheld, either before, during or after the making of the film." This remark is curious, considering Buckner's involvement in the script, either enhancing the mystery of Roemheld's contribution or illustrating Buckner's distance from the project once it entered the production stages.

58. Quoted from McGilligan, *Cagney: The Actor as Auteur*, pp. 94–95.

## Postscript

But the critic—the audience of one—who concerned the Cagneys most was George M. Cohan. Confined to his Fifth Avenue apartment during the filming of *Dandy*, Cohan knew that the approved screenplay-in-progress was being rewritten without his input, and his lawyers protested to the nervous Warners front office. In California, his representative was Ed Raftery, "300 pounds of amiable Irishman who was nevertheless under strict orders to pounce on anything he knew Cohan wouldn't like."[59] William Cagney persuaded Raftery, who was president of United Artists as well as a lawyer, to wait until the Cagneys could assemble a rough cut. At the screening for Raftery, "bulky Ed sat at one end of a long lounge for the viewing, and my 220-pound brother sat at the other."[60] Cagney tells the rest of the story: "Inasmuch as the script had not been submitted to Cohan, my brother was full of misgivings, feeling the lawyer friend would step all over it. My brother was wrong. About twenty minutes into the film it really got to Mr. Raftery. As he sat on the other end of the room, my brother could feel the lounge vibrating as he realized Mr. Raftery was crying. Bill knew he was home free then."[61]

Cohan himself saw the finished *Dandy* sometime later. A projector, screen, and print of the movie were delivered to Cohan and his wife at their summer home in Monroe, New York, where they finally saw *Dandy* in a hall over the town firehouse at the end of April 1942. During the screening Cohan had to be escorted from the room several times to relieve himself, so badly was he now suffering from cancer of the bladder. After the lights went up, according to an apocryphal anecdote related by Cagney, Mrs. Cohan, who had not risen out of her wheelchair for years, got up and walked over to George M. and said, "George, you were fine." Writes Cagney: "She had accepted me as George so completely. Now that may be all fraudulent, but I thought you should know it. It is interesting if true." Then Co-

59. Cagney, *Cagney by Cagney*, p. 106.
60. Cagney, *Cagney by Cagney*, p. 107.
61. Cagney to McGilligan, July 3, 1979.

han sent Cagney a brief telegram: "Dear Jim, How's my double? Thanks for a wonderful job. Sincerely, George M. Cohan."[62]
McCabe describes Cohan's final months:

By late summer of 1942, his weakness was pronounced, but one eve-ning he announced to his nurse a determination to take a ride down Broadway. She argued, but he was adamant. They drove down Fifth Avenue, through Times Square and the theatre district, stopping briefly at the southeast corner of Broadway and 43rd Street to look at the movie house which had once been the George M. Cohan Theatre. Then down to 14th Street to the site of Tony Pastor's Music Hall, then to Union Square where the Four Cohans had made their New York debut, finally back uptown to the Hollywood Theatre (now the Mark Hellinger Theatre) where Cohan and his nurse sat in the back row, unnoticed, to watch a few minutes of *Yankee Doodle Dandy*. Cohan smiled as he heard the actor playing President Roosevelt and James Cagney speak two of the very few lines Cohan actually wrote for the film which were retained in the script: "Where else in the world could a plain guy like me sit down and talk things over with the head man?"; "Well now, you know, Mr. Cohan, that's as good a definition of America as I've ever heard."[63] In Cohan's view, it made a pretty good ending to a pretty good picture. As "Over There," the last number in the film, was playing, he walked out of the theatre and was driven back to his apartment. He had given his last regards to Broadway.

On the evening of November 4, it was apparent that he was slipping into a coma. To his bedside in his apartment at 993 Fifth Avenue came Monsignor John J. Casey, representing Archbishop Spellman, and Father Francis X. Shea, to administer the last rites of the Roman Catho-lic Church. Just before he lost consciousness, Cohan spoke his last words, "Look after Agnes." She was there, together with Cohan's chil-dren, Georgette, Mary, Helen, and George M., Jr. As the dawn was breaking on November 5, 1942, Mary Cohan, holding her father's hand, felt it go limp. He had gone easily, without pain.[64]

62. Cagney to McGilligan, July 3, 1979.

63. Actually, it is unclear whether Cohan *did* write these two lines, which so perfectly embody the patriotic sentiment of *Dandy*. They appear practically ver-batim in Buckner's first draft, the Screenplay and Outline (June 12–19, 1941), although they may have been suggested by Cohan during his conversations in New York with Buckner two months earlier (transcript dated April 3, 1941).

64. McCabe, *George M. Cohan*, pp. 266–67.

It may be that the last word on her father belongs more appropriately to Georgette Cohan, the daughter of Ethel Levey and George M., who is said to have remarked of *Dandy*, "That's the kind of a life daddy would have liked to have lived."[65] Cohan had kept up with the rhapsodic reviews, the accumulating box-office statistics. *Dandy* was all the legacy he could have hoped for, an untarnished image for all time. Even *Variety*, which had had its occasional quarrels with the song-and-dance artist, reported his death with an outpouring of goodwill: "A great little guy cashed in his chips yesterday. He was ever with the world. He did his stuff and did it well. A little guy born on the 4th of July."

65. Ward Morehouse, *George M. Cohan: Prince of the American Theater* (New York: Lippincott, 1943), p. 229.

1. *George (James Cagney) gets an "early evening" summons.*

2. *"Well, all signs point to its being a boy."*

3. *Little Georgie (Henry Blair) as "The Dancing Master."*

4. *The Four Cohans in blackface, from vaudeville montage.*

5. *Buffalo gal (Joan Leslie) and bewhiskered George.*

6. *George and Josie (Jeanne Cagney), from "I Was Born in Virginia."*

7. *"My mother thanks you, my father thanks you, my sister thanks you . . ."*

8. *"The Warmest Baby in the Bunch."*

9. *"H-A-double R-I-G-A-N spells Harrigan."*

10. *Schwab (S. Z. Sakall) launches the Cohan and Harris partnership.*

11. *Defying gravity, from "Yankee Doodle Dandy."*

12. *Waiting for the skyrocket in* Little Johnny Jones.

13. *"Give My Regards to Broadway."*

14. *The Three Cohans in the waiting room of a railroad station.*

15. *Reunited, from "The Barber's Ball" montage.*

16. *"Mary's a Grand Old Name."*

17. *"Fay has the song, but I have the author."*

18. *The encounter between George and Foy (Eddie Foy, Jr.).*

19. *Democracy tableau from* George Washington, Jr.

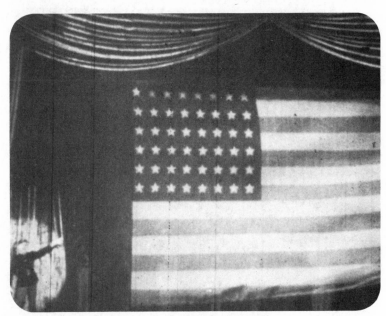

20. *"You're a Grand Old Flag."*

21. *Josie retires from the Four Cohans, "just a simple case of subtraction."*

22. *Jerry Cohan's (Walter Huston) sixty-second birthday.*

23. *Montage from "Over There."*

24. *Singer (Frances Langford) and George at army camp.*

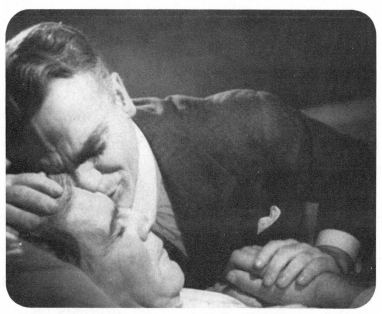

25. *George weeps at the death of his father.*

26. *The dissolution of the Cohan-Harris partnership.*

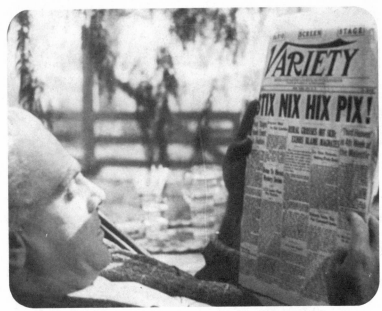

27. *George in retirement, down on the farm.*

28. *"No other actor in the world but you could do it."*

29. *"Off the Record" from* I'd Rather Be Right.

30. *The Oval Office after George's departure.*

31. *George tap-dances down the White House stairs.*

32. *George, in step with World War II patriotism, sings "Over There."*

# Yankee Doodle Dandy

Screenplay

by

ROBERT BUCKNER

and

EDMUND JOSEPH

Additional material by

JULIUS and PHILIP EPSTEIN

Original Story by

ROBERT BUCKNER

# Yankee Doodle Dandy

## Prologue

FADE IN

A.    FULL SHOT   A HUGE ELECTRIC SIGN ON THEATER (INSERT)
The biggest sign on Broadway, sparkling with a border
of red, white, and blue lights, proclaims to the world:

SAM H. HARRIS PRESENTS
GEORGE M. COHAN
in his triumphal return to the stage
in
*I'd Rather Be Right*
The Greatest Musical Comedy Hit in Years

CAMERA PANS DOWN TO:

B.    SRO SIGN
on box office. PAN OVER to large picture of George M.
Cohan on easel or in frame.[1]

DISSOLVE TO:

C.    INT. COHAN'S DRESSING ROOM
Cohan, Mary, Harris, and a group of friends are present. Cohan's back is to the audience as he talks to the
backslappers and well-wishers. Mary is opening a batch
of telegrams. Harris is in the process of opening a bottle
of champagne.

GEORGE:
> It's all very well, but I'm still worried. Lot of people
> won't like it—imitating the president of the United
> States!

ONE OF THE BACKSLAPPERS:
> It's all in good, clean fun. And didn't they love it in
> Boston?

83

MARY:

> The greatest man in the United States played by the greatest actor. There's nothing wrong in that. Especially when the greatest actor is my husband.

George turns around. He looks just like FDR.

GEORGE:

> Still—it's wartime. It may be treason. I may get shot for this.

The friends laugh, start to leave.

ONE OF THE FRIENDS (as he goes):

> Don't worry. I know a dollar-a-year man who'll take care of you.

GEORGE:

> I bet they'd love to shoot actors. It's good machine gun practice . . . Thanks a lot for dropping in.

The last of the friends are gone now. George picks up a bunch of telegrams, goes through them.

MARY (as she reads a telegram):

> Oh, here's the one I sent you. It's very clever.

George is smiling broadly now as he reads the congratulatory telegrams.

HARRIS (still opening the bottle):

> Don't forget. Save the telegrams. The government needs the paper.

Suddenly, as George glances at another telegram, the happy grin vanishes from his face.

GEORGE (groaning):

> Oh—

MARY:

> What's the matter?

GEORGE (gulps):

> Here—read this!

He hands her the wire.

D.    CLOSE-UP   MARY
as she reads the wire aloud.

E.    INSERT   THE TELEGRAM   IN MARY'S HANDS
It reads:

> WASHINGTON, D.C.
>
> GEORGE M. COHAN
> ALVIN THEATER, N.Y. CITY
> THE PRESIDENT OF THE UNITED STATES REQUESTS
> THAT YOU CALL UPON HIM AT YOUR EARLIEST CONVE-
> NIENCE IN REGARD TO A PERSONAL MATTER. KINDLY
> REPLY FOR DEFINITE APPOINTMENT AT WHITE HOUSE.
> SECRETARY TO THE PRESIDENT

F.    MED. CLOSE   THREE SHOT   GEORGE, MARY, AND SAM
HARRIS
All three of them are staring fixedly at the ominous message and all completely oblivious of the excitement
around them. Slowly George looks up at Sam Harris.

GEORGE (trying to hide his anxiety):
> They can't shoot me. I've got a run-of-the-play con-
> tract.

At this moment Harris opens the champagne bottle
with a loud *pop!* George starts back with fright.[2]
DISSOLVE TO:

G–H.   OMITTED

I.    EXT. PENNSYLVANIA AVENUE   WASHINGTON, D.C.   NIGHT
Cohan, his coat collar turned up against the light drizzle
of rain and the brim of his hat slanted over one eye, is
walking along the street.[3] He stops when he comes to
the gates of the White House. Of course, there are fully
armed soldiers guarding it. One of them immediately
challenges George.

85

SOLDIER:
> Yeah? What do you want?

GEORGE:
> I have an appointment.

SOLDIER:
> What's the name?

GEORGE:
> Cohan. George M. Cohan.[4]

SOLDIER (the name means nothing to him):
> You step back a minute. I'll call.

DISSOLVE TO:

J–K.  INT. THE WHITE HOUSE  FOYER  FULL SHOT
Cohan's hat and coat are taken by an elderly, white-haired Negro butler, and Cohan looks around him with respectful interest. This is one of the greatest moments of his crowded life. The Negro butler returns from the cloakroom and starts toward the stairway. He is a very likable character.

NEGRO BUTLER (courteously):
> Will you follow me, please, sir?[5]

Cohan nods nervously and the CAMERA PANS with them as they cross the foyer, then start up the broad marble stairway to the second floor. In the early evening hour the White House is impressively quiet and still.

L.  DOLLY SHOT  UP THE STAIRWAY
As Cohan and the Negro butler ascend the steps, Cohan glances at the rows of framed portraits which line the walls, the stern-faced American statesmen of the past, the heroic generals and admirals.

NEGRO BUTLER (hesitantly):
> I was s'posed to be off duty tonight, Mr. Cohan, but when I heard you was comin', I—(he grins.)

Well, sir, I just wanted to see if you still looked the same.

GEORGE (amused):
That sort of depends on when you saw me last, don't it?

NEGRO BUTLER (reflecting):
It musta been thirty-some years ago. I was valet for Mr. "Teddy" Roosevelt and he got me a seat up in the gallery . . . The play was *George Washin'ton, Jr.* You was dancin' and singin' about the grand ole flag. (Chuckles.) Mr. Teddy used to sing it in his bathtub.

Cohan smiles as they turn at the first landing and continue up the next flight of steps.

GEORGE:
That was a pretty good old song in its day.

NEGRO BUTLER:
Yas, sir. And it's just as good today as it *ever* was.

The CAMERA PANS with them as they go up to the door of the president's private study. A footman walks past, carrying several pieces of luggage up the hall.

NEGRO BUTLER (to George):
Mrs. Roosevelt has just come in from Atlanta.[6]

The butler knocks on the door and a voice from within the room replies for the caller to enter. The butler turns the knob and holds the door open for Cohan to enter.

M.    MED. TRUCK SHOT    COHAN    FROM INT. STUDY
The CAMERA is inside the study, HOLDING on the doorway as Cohan enters. The CAMERA PULLS BACK with him as he approaches the desk, then pauses, waiting.

N.    WIDER ANGLE    THE STUDY
The president is seated at his desk, signing a sheaf of

papers and smoking a cigarette in a black holder. On one corner of the desk a tray contains his unfinished dinner. The beautiful paneled room, oval in shape, its walls covered with old naval prints, is softly lighted by a single lamp on the president's desk and also by the birch logs which are crackling cheerfully in the fireplace.

The president looks suddenly up from his work, smiles cordially at his nervous visitor, and extends his hand across the desk.

PRESIDENT:

Well, hello there! How's my double?

GEORGE (embarrassed, shaking hands):

I—I wouldn't know how to answer that one, Mr. President.

PRESIDENT:

No? (Chuckles.) Why, I was told that you knew all the answers.

GEORGE (grins sheepishly):

I only wish I did.

PRESIDENT (sighs):

Yes, so do I. (Gestures to chair.) Sit down, Mr. Cohan.

GEORGE:

Thanks. (Starts to sit down, but in his nervousness bumps the chair.) I'm a little nervous.

The president laughs and Cohan relaxes under the power of the famous personality.

PRESIDENT:

I'm sorry I missed the opening. Tell me, Mr. Cohan, how do you feel about playing me on the stage?

GEORGE:

Well, right this minute, not so good. How do *you* feel about it?

PRESIDENT (laughs good-naturedly):
　　I'd like to see the show. I've always thought you
　　were a great actor.

GEORGE:
　　Thanks. That's a great compliment coming from
　　you.

The president takes this amusedly and looks over his
glasses at George with kidding severity.

PRESIDENT:
　　Now see here—just how am I to take that?

GEORGE (flustered at his faux pas):
　　Oh, don't misunderstand me, Mr. President. I
　　meant—

The president laughs and waves it aside, interrupting
George's attempted explanations.

PRESIDENT:
　　Don't worry about it. We understand each other
　　perfectly. (He sits back and lights a cigarette.) You
　　know, I remember you and your family very well—
　　the Four Cohans—

GEORGE (interested):
　　Do you, Mr. President? That was a long time ago.

PRESIDENT:
　　Yes, it was when I was going to school near Bos-
　　ton.[7]

GEORGE (smiles):
　　I was a pretty cocky kid in those days—a regular
　　Yankee Doodle Dandy. Always *in* a parade or fol-
　　lowing one.

PRESIDENT:
　　I hope you haven't outgrown the habit.

GEORGE:

Not a chance. Even if I tried to, I don't think the public would let me.

PRESIDENT:

That's one thing I've always admired about you Irish-Americans. You carry your love of country like a flag, right out in the open. It's a great quality.

GEORGE:

I guess I got it from my father. He ran off to the Civil War at thirteen—the proudest kid in the state of Massachusetts.

PRESIDENT (chuckles):

So you've spent your life telling the other forty-seven states what a great country it is.

0.       CLOSE-UP   GEORGE

He smiles thoughtfully, hesitating a moment before re-plying.

GEORGE:

Well, sir, I never thought of it just that way—but I guess it's true. Maybe it all started with a funny thing that happened about sixty years ago . . .[8]

SLOW DISSOLVE TO:

FADE IN

1.       EXT. STREET PARADE   LONG SHOT                  DAY

The scene is a Fourth of July parade down the main street of a typical American city of sixty years ago. The sidewalks are lined with crowds watching the colorful but motley collection of marching men, who include the inevitable local fire brigade with their red and brass pump engines, the police force with their "thunder-mug" helmets, and a considerable company of patriotic citizens, each carrying a small American flag. A large brass band, handsomely uniformed, is blaring forth a military march tune of the period. The storefronts are gaily decorated with large flags and red, white, and blue streamers. Everyone is having a very good time. OVER THIS SHOT comes Cohan's voice, as if continuing from the previous scene.

GEORGE'S VOICE:
> It was the Fourth of July, 1878 . . . in Providence, Rhode Island . . .[9]

2.  LONG DOLLY OR BOOM SHOT ·
The CAMERA MOVES STRAIGHT THROUGH THE PARADE to the opposite side of the street, and above the crowd on the sidewalk to the ornate front of an old-fashioned theater, finally to HOLD on the billboard which bears the names of the various acts in the program being performed within. They include McIntyre & Heath, Trebor, the Man of Mystic Changes, Captain McCrosson's Zouaves, Ned Oliver and His Banjo, and one or two other famous variety acts of the seventies. The sound of the brass band from the street and the cheering of the crowd continues OVER THE SHOT.

3.  CLOSE-UP   THEATER BILLBOARD   INSERT
The top number on the bill reads:
> MR. & MRS. JERRY COHAN
> "The Irish Darlings"

OVER THIS SHOT we again hear Cohan's voice, with a note of genuine affection.

GEORGE'S VOICE:
> My father was playing there in a variety theater, and my mother should have been with him on the stage . . . but she was busy right then in a smaller production . . .
>
> DISSOLVE THROUGH BILLBOARD TO:

4.  CLOSE PANNING SHOT   JERRY COHAN'S FEET   ON
STAGE   INT. THEATER
Only the buckled shoes, white stockings, and buttoned-

top knee britches of a typical Irish trouper of the 1870s are visible in the SHOT. But they are dancing with considerable skill a lively jig, accompanied by the fast music of a small orchestra.

CAMERA PULLS BACK TO:

5.    FULL PANNING SHOT   JERRY COHAN   ON STAGE
George's father is a handsome young man of slightly above average height, with an immediately likable face and manner. His costume, in addition to the items described above, consists of a braid-faced coat with a short cape attached, a fancy waistcoat, and a jaunty Irish hat. Photographs available of this. His dance routine is very clever and amusing. Suddenly he "breaks" as the orchestra slides into his specialty song, "The Dancing Master."

As he pauses singing and does another brief jig, we hear a burst of appreciative laughter and applause from the audience, off-scene. No actual audience is needed for this scene.

6.    CLOSE MOVING SHOT   JERRY COHAN   ON STAGE
This closer view of George's father reveals a strangely worried look in his eyes, an anxious distraction, as if his mind were not upon his act. He glances toward the wings as he hits the chorus. When he finishes, he flashes the audience a quick, automatic smile, and then without waiting for the applause that follows, he runs hurriedly across the stage and disappears into the wings.

7.    FULL SHOT   BACKSTAGE   PANNING
As Jerry Cohan runs into the wings he confronts tensely a colorful group that includes other actors, waiting for their turns on the stage, and the stage manager. The actors, both men and women, wear an interesting variety of costumes and makeups, all of the 1870 vintage.

JERRY COHAN (excitedly):
> Has any message come for me?

AN ACTRESS:
> Not a word yet, Jerry.

As the group looks at him with amused smiles, Jerry turns quickly to the stage manager.

JERRY COHAN:
> Max—I can't wait! I've got to go and find out what's happening!

He runs toward stage door.

STAGE MANAGER:
> You can't run through the streets in *that* outfit—and with makeup on. They'll throw you into jail.

JERRY COHAN (wildly):
> They'll have to catch me first.

He continues to race toward the stage door. The actors and the stage manager look after him with affectionate smiles.

ACTORS:
> Good luck, Jerry! Give her a kiss for me! Bring us the news!

STAGE MANAGER (yells):
> Remember—you're on again at four-fifteen, Jerry!

There is prolonged applause from the audience, off-scene.

8.    FULL SHOT   JERRY COHAN   AT STAGE DOOR
As he jerks open the door, he turns for a second and yells back.

JERRY COHAN:
> Somebody take that bow for me!

He vanishes through the doorway.[10]

9.     EXT. PARADE IN STREET   FULL SHOT   PANNING

Still in his comical makeup, Jerry Cohan runs out of the theater alley and into the crowd on the sidewalk, so solidly packed that they block his way. The CAMERA FOLLOWS HIM as he forces a path through them, his face filled with anxiety. Some of the crowd give him a startled look as he brushes past.

10.    FULL TRUCKING SHOT   IN THE PARADE

Right behind the band marches a blue-uniformed collection of Civil War veterans, men about forty-five years of age and strutting with patriotic pride. One is carrying a large gold-fringed American flag and behind him two others support a widespread banner with the sign:

VETERANS OF THE G.A.R.
LOCAL NO. 3

Right in back of the men is a Civil War cannon, the caisson being pulled by the usual team of artillery horses.

Jerry Cohan tries to cross the street directly through the parade, but gets caught between the lines of marching ex-soldiers, who look in surprise at his remarkable getup.

JERRY COHAN (tensely):
Excuse me, boys. Can I get through here, please?

A VETERAN (points helpfully):
The Irish are up at the head of the parade—as usual.[11]

JERRY COHAN (struggling to get through):
*I'm* not in this parade! I'm—

But the band music flares up louder than usual and Jerry can't make himself heard. The veterans look at him blankly. Finally Jerry reaches up, shouts something into one of the veteran's ears.

VETERAN:
Oh! Why didn't you say so? We'll get you there in no time!

He lifts Jerry up, seats him on the artillery caisson.

VETERAN (to the horses):
    Charge!

The horses dash away in very military fashion, as the onlookers stare.

DISSOLVE TO:

11.    INT. THE BOARDING HOUSE    FULL SHOT    THE COHANS'
       ROOM
       The room is large and comfortable, but old-fashioned. A woman lies in the big double bed with a newborn baby swaddled in the curve of her arm. An elderly doctor and a woman nurse are packing up their medical equipment. The baby is crying in no uncertain manner. From the street outside, the distant band music is continuous over this scene. Suddenly the door bursts open and Jerry Cohan rushes in, tensely excited and looking very amusing in his theatrical costume. His heavy Irish wig has slipped over one ear and he is holding the flag in his hand. His eyes go straight to his wife, in apprehension.

JERRY COHAN (softly):
    Nellie!

12.    CLOSE SHOT    NELLIE COHAN    IN BED
       George's mother is a very good-looking young woman, though just now, of course, she is somewhat pale and drawn. She opens her eyes to look at her husband and smiles faintly.

13.    FULL SHOT    CENTER OF THE ROOM
       Jerry Cohan looks anxiously at the doctor and nurse, who are both smiling.

JERRY COHAN:
    Is she all right?

The doctor nods and Jerry peers back at the stranger in
his bed, too excited to know what he is saying.

JERRY COHAN:
    What—is it, Doc?

DOCTOR (dryly):
    Well—all signs point to its being a boy.[12]

Jerry Cohan's face beams at the good news and he
walks in awe toward the bed.

14.     MED. SHOT    MOTHER AND BABY    AT BED
Nellie Cohan's happy eyes follow her husband as he
comes up INTO THE SHOT and stands beside the bed. He
presses her hand silently but in a way that speaks his
love, then for the first time he looks at his son, who is
now sleeping soundly.

JERRY COHAN:
    What? He's just got here. Sleeping already?

NELLIE COHAN (softly):
    All babies sleep twenty hours a day, Jerry.

JERRY COHAN:
    It's no wonder most of them never amount to any-
    thing. (Looks down proudly at his son.) What'll we
    call him?

The old doctor comes up slowly INTO THE SHOT and
joins them, buttoning his starched cuffs.

DOCTOR:
    Seeing that he arrived on the Fourth of July, what
    about George Washington Cohan?

The mother smiles, but the father is intrigued.

JERRY COHAN:
    Mmm—nice, patriotic ring to it— (To his wife.)
    What do you think, darling?

NELLIE COHAN (thoughtfully):
Well—the George is fine—but the Washington—
may be too long for a billboard.

JERRY COHAN:
Uh-huh. How about a good short Irish name. Dennis—or Michael?

Nellie Cohan looks down at the bundle containing her
son.

NELLIE COHAN (slowly):
George—Michael—Cohan. (She looks up and
smiles.) Yes—I like that name.

Young George awakens and starts to bawl lustily.

NELLIE COHAN (reproachfully):
Oh, Jerry—

JERRY COHAN (straightens up suddenly):
Heavenly day, Nellie—he's crying with a brogue!

Over the sound track comes the voice of George M. Cohan, as before, while the CAMERA HOLDS on the family
group.

GEORGE'S VOICE:
And probably the first thing I ever held was the
American flag. It was six or seven years later before
I realized they weren't celebrating *my* birthday on
the Fourth of July . . . I had a kid sister by then—
Josie—who took after me in everything. We had the
same love for show business—and gosh, how we
both hated school—[13]

DISSOLVE TO:

15. INT. A MOVING TRAIN DOLLY SHOT
Late at night on a "sleeper jump," a group of typical
vaudeville actors are riding in an old-style red plush
day coach with swaying gas lights.

16.  MED. GROUP SHOT   THE FOUR COHANS
     They sit in facing seats. Young George is apparently
     asleep beside his father, while Josie is curled up in her
     mother's lap, also asleep. Their battered luggage rests
     on the racks above their heads.

JERRY (worriedly):
>    But they won't *stay* in any school. We've tried it
>    three times. They think any other life except show
>    business is a form of punishment.

NELLIE:
>    That's because you've never been firm with George.
>    It's the old story, Jerry. Spare the rod and spoil the
>    child.

JERRY:
>    I agree with that absolutely—but I think it's the
>    mother's place—

NELLIE (shocked):
>    Mother's place? Are you suggesting that I raise a
>    hand against a darling child I brought into this
>    world? You know very well it's a father's duty—

JERRY (doggedly):
>    It's my theory—the hand that rocks the cradle
>    should wield the rod.

NELLIE:
>    The trouble with you, Jerry Cohan, is you're too
>    soft-hearted—

JERRY (looks fondly down on George):
>    Nellie—how much have we saved this season?
>    'Bout seven hundred dollars, isn't it? That would
>    do it.

NELLIE:
>    Do what?

JERRY (it's a big moment in the Four Cohans' lives):
Put our own show on the road!

NELLIE (dazed):
Our *own* show!?

JERRY (enthusiastically):
Yes—I've got a great idea! George can do a violin act—Josie can do her skirt dancing—and you and I'll do a couple of sketches. For a finish I'll write a one-act play for the four of us.

Her eyes eager with excitement, Nellie is speechless for a moment. But suddenly young George opens one bright eye, then answers excitedly.

GEORGE:
Oh, boy! That's *wonderful!*

His parents look down at him quickly, then at each other and burst out laughing. His father hugs him close as the train with its swinging gas lights rattles on through the night.[14]

DISSOLVE TO:

17.  MONTAGE[15]

1. EXT. A THEATRICAL BILLBOARD (INSERT)   CLOSE SHOT
DAY
A twenty-four-sheet stand of bills, amusingly illustrated in the old-time style, boldly proclaims:
AMERICA'S FAVORITE FAMILY OF ENTERTAINERS
"THE COHAN MIRTH-MAKERS"
The Celebrated Troupe of Singers, Dancers,
and Comedians,
with their Silver-Plated Band
FOR ONE NIGHT ONLY IN PEORIA
OVER THIS SHOT comes the sound of band music blaring out Sousa's "Gladiator March."

DISSOLVE TO:

2. INT. A THEATER CLOSE SHOT AN "ACT" SIGN ON STAGE

The dazzling silvery letters on a blue velvet background read:

MASTER GEORGIE

Violin Tricks & Tinkling Tunes

CAMERA PANS AWAY to the stage where George, wearing a fancy white-embroidered suit, is playing "Carnival in Venice," no less, on a small violin—not in the normal position, but above his head and then between his legs!

QUICK DISSOLVE TO:

3. CLOSE SHOT THE "ACT" SIGN ON STAGE

As Master Georgie's banner is flipped back we read in spangly letters on the next sign:

LITTLE JOSIE COHAN

America's Youngest Skirt Dancer

CAMERA PANS AWAY to the stage where Josie, encrusted with curls and ruffles, is dancing a solo number with much skill and grace, and to much applause from the off-scene audience.

DISSOLVE TO:

4. INSERT THE COHAN FAMILY ALBUM

As the pages turn with the passing years we see Nellie Cohan's hands inserting new pictures of the family group and of George and Josie. Music is behind these shots and we superimpose the years—1888, 1889, 1890. The last picture in the album is one of the new thirteen-year-old George and eleven-year-old Josie in their amusing dancing-doll costumes for "Goggles Doll House."[16]

LAP DISSOLVE TO:

5. INT. A THEATER TOWARD THE STAGE "DANCING DOLL" ACT

The Four Cohans are performing their "Goggles Doll House" act on the stage of an old-fashioned theater, to the gay music of the piece. OVER THIS WE DOUBLE-EXPOSE the names of famous old theaters: B. F. Keith's, the Hippodrome, Austin and Stone's Museum, the Four Cohans in "Goggles Doll House."

GEORGE'S VOICE (comes over the above montage):
>It was a great life but a hard one—year after year of one-night stands, early jumps, and bad hotels. We boiled in summer and froze in winter. But to a stagestruck kid like me it was heaven on wheels . . . In 1891 we were broke and stranded, when suddenly out of the blue came a great offer that saved our lives . . .
>>DISSOLVE TO:

18.    EXT THE BROOKLYN THEATER                          DAY
A huge illustrated billboard which reads in bold letters:
THE FOUR COHANS
in
*Peck's Bad Boy*
OVER THIS comes the sound of voices from the crowd and music.

19.    INSERT    A GILT STAR
which is being nailed to a door.

JERRYS VOICE (OVER insert):
>What do they mean hammering on our opening night? I'll go blank—I won't be able to remember a line . . .

The CAMERA PULLS BACK and we see George, dressed in his Peck's Bad Boy outfit on a stage ladder, hammering a gilt star on the door. As the door is yanked open, he almost falls off the ladder.

JERRY (as he rushes to steady the teetering ladder):
>What are you doing up there!

GEORGE:
>I'm the star of this play, ain't I?

JERRY:
> Well—you've got the leading part.

GEORGE:
> That means I'm a star. And if I'm a star, there
> should be a star on my dressing room door. That's
> the law of the theater, Dad—

As Jerry is about to explode, Nellie intervenes.

NELLIE (smiling):
> Yes, Jerry. Give the devil his due.

The stage manager comes into the scene.

STAGE MANAGER (at the top of his voice):
> Places, please! Curtain going up!

George's calm and cockiness deserts him suddenly.

GEORGE (very nervous now):
> Oh—

He sways and falls off the ladder into his father's arms.

NELLIE (she and Josie run forward):
> George! [17]

DISSOLVE TO:

20.  THE "PECK'S BAD BOY" ROUTINE
The play is covered with the following MONTAGE SHOTS,
INTERCUTTING between the actors and the reactions of
the audience, to establish both George's and the play's
success.

1. AT THE WINGS The Four Cohans are wishing each
other Godspeed.[18]

NELLIE (shaking hands with George):
> Good luck, George. (She kisses Josie.) Josie!

JERRY:
> Do your best, son—and don't be nervous.

GEORGE:
    Me, nervous? (He is.)

Josie and Nellie kiss. Josie tries to kiss George, but he pushes away from her.

GEORGE:
    Aw!

2. DOUBLE EXPOSURE
Hands applaud over a program of *Peck's Bad Boy*.
                                    LAP DISSOLVE TO:

3. THE PLAY    INT. SCHULTZ GROCERY STORE
The irate Schultz is chasing Henry Peck around the store. Henry, to get away from him, jumps up on a flour barrel. Its top collapses. Schultz makes a lunge for him. Henry grabs him by the coattail and spins him around. Schultz reels around the store and, to keep from falling, he grabs the window blind—it falls.
                                    LAP DISSOLVE TO:

4. SHOTS OF LAUGHING HEADS
                                    LAP DISSOLVE TO:

5. ALBEE
of Keith and Albee, who is taking in the show. (He is a tough New Englander, about forty-four years old.) He looks through his program, then puts his finger on the name George M. Cohan.
                                    LAP DISSOLVE TO:

6. THE PLAY (CONTINUED)
Schultz is still trying to lay his hands on Henry Peck. The Irish cop comes rushing in to try and help Schultz catch Henry. Henry goes over to a crate of tomatoes and starts pelting both of them with the overripe fruit. They give chase. Henry climbs up on several crates of eggs, takes one, and dumps it on the cop and storekeeper. In order to keep from falling, Henry grabs at the shelving; the whole thing comes down and tin cans virtually

cover the cop and storekeeper. Henry towers over them, a devilish grin on his face.

HENRY:

I can lick any kid in town.[19]

LAP DISSOLVE TO:

7. THE TOWN'S TOUGH KIDS IN THE BALCONY
They are watching intently, judging the badness of Peck's Bad Boy. They look at each other scornfully.

LAP DISSOLVE TO:

21.    FULL DOLLY SHOT    BACKSTAGE
Flushed and excited from his personal triumph, George enters from his last curtain. The actors crowd around him.

ACTORS (ad lib):

Nice going, kid! Congratulations! That was a real piece of acting, Georgie! I didn't know you had it in you, boy!

All of these congratulations naturally come together. George takes the backslapping and handshaking with a look of amused wonder as the CAMERA FOLLOWS the group.

GEORGE (very chesty):

Thanks—but what are you all so surprised about? You could've told during rehearsals that I'd be a sensation in this part. (The family are thunder-struck—stop dead in their tracks. The other actors and backstage crew glance at each other.) Listen, there's nothing to this acting business. I wonder what took me so long to become a star.

22.    JERRY AND NELLIE
in the wings. They are listening to George's speech.

NELLIE:

Jerry—the time has come for George's first spank-ing.

JERRY:

You're right, Nellie. I'll hold him while you hit him.

NELLIE:

Not me. I don't hit hard enough to make an impression.

JERRY:

Well, I can't do it. He'll think I'm just jealous because he got more laughs than I did— (Pause, smiles.) And don't think I'm not.

23.   GEORGE AND ACTORS

George is still holding forth, going toward dressing room.

GEORGE:

I think you boys could brush up a bit on your performance. Maybe we'd better rehearse tomorrow morning and I'll put you through your paces—

The stage manager comes into the scene.

STAGE MANAGER (smiling queerly):

Several gentlemen to see you outside, *Mr.* Cohan.

GEORGE:

Oh—gentlemen of the press, I presume. It's starting already. Will you excuse me?

He swaggers toward the stage door.

24.   JERRY

watching him, perturbed. Then he slams the dressing room door shut behind him. The star, only half nailed on, falls to the floor.

25.   EXT. THE THEATER ALLEY

There is a group of boys lounging against a fence, the same six hoodlums we saw in the theater gallery. George comes out, looks around for the newspapermen. One of the hoodlums calls out:

HOODLUM:

Here he is, fellers. Let's see how tough he is!

Whereupon they all pounce upon him, fists swinging.

DISSOLVE TO:

26.   INT. THE COHANS' DRESSING ROOM

SHOOTING INTO A MIRROR as George, seated in front of it, receives anxious first aid from his mother and sister, Josie, who are trying to restore his ruined grandeur with water and cloths. George's nose is bloody, his lip cut, and one eye is rapidly closing with the blue "mouse." His hair and clothes are badly disheveled and he is fighting mad as a bantam rooster.

NELLIE:

They ought to be arrested, every one of those hoodlums! (Turns on Jerry.) And it seems to me, Jerry Cohan, you're taking all this very calmly. When your only son is almost murdered in cold—

JERRY (calmly):

The way I look at it, it's a fine tribute to Georgie's acting. The way he plays it, every tough kid in America will want to take a punch at Peck's Bad Boy, just to see what happens.

GEORGE (excitedly):

*What!* Have I got to go through this *every* night!?

JERRY:

And matinees, Wednesday and Saturday. (Quietly.) Georgie—those boys did you a great favor—and they saved me some trouble. (George stares at his father wonderingly, as do his mother and sister.) Most actors give their whole lives to their profession without once scoring a hit. You're lucky; you're a hit at the age of thirteen. You're going to be a big star, there's no doubt about that. You're going to be surrounded by a lot of admirers and backslappers—but you're going to have very few friends. The way you treated your fellow actors a little while ago will take care of that. Those kids in the street gave you a good idea of what a performer means to the public. What friends—real friends— mean to a performer you'll have to find out for yourself. I've been in this profession a long time but I never ran across a performer who, in the long run, wouldn't rather be a great guy than a great actor. That is—until I made your acquaintance.

GEORGE (shaken):

Can't—c-can't I be both?

JERRY:

The chances are, that if you keep on the way you are, you won't be either. If the hoodlums won't get you, a committee of actors will! Actors are considered pretty bad risks by insurance companies, but an actor with a conceit like yours—well, we couldn't afford the premium!

NELLIE (softening the blow):

What your father really means—is that you're too sensitive, too anxious to make good—you love the theater too much. I know you can cure yourself, if you want to.[20]

GEORGE (emotionally):

Sure I can. Just watch me. From now on I'm Peck's Bad Boy only from eight-thirty till eleven in the evenings.

JOSIE:

And Wednesdays and Saturdays—two-thirty till five.

GEORGE:

Yes, sir. The other twenty-one and a half hours I pattern myself after Pop. (He extends his hand to his father.)

JERRY (taking his hand):
> Well—you can find a better example—but that's the
> general idea—

Solemnly the two shake hands, and there are tears of
happiness in Nellie's and Josie's eyes. Suddenly the
door is flung open and one of the actors we saw backstage strides in.

ACTOR (in a great state of excitement):
> What do you know? Ed Albee is coming backstage
> to see you!

And he strides right out again. The news creates a sensation among the Cohans.

NELLIE:
> Albee! That's B. F. Keith's partner!

JERRY:
> That means big time vaudeville. Nellie, we're in the
> big time!

NELLIE:
> And he didn't send for us! *He's* coming *here* to see
> us!

GEORGE (importantly):
> Dad, maybe it would be better if I spoke business
> to him.

JOSIE (reproachfully):
> Georgie! I thought you said you were going to re-
> form!

JERRY (to George):
> I don't want to hear a word out of you when he's
> here. (Looks around.) Look at the condition of this
> dressing room!

A frantic cleanup starts.

NELLIE:
> Get the cheap makeup off the table!

27. **DOOR**
as it is flung open again and another excited actor sticks his head in.

**SECOND ACTOR:**
Albee'll be right in. He stopped at the water cooler.

He bangs the door shut behind him.

**NELLIE:**
Jerry, if he offers you a cigar, don't take it!

**GEORGE:**
I'll take it. It'll impress him if he thinks I can smoke.

Father and mother turn to look at him.

**JERRY** (as approaching footsteps are heard):
Georgie—get behind that curtain. (He indicates curtain which screens off the women's side of the room.)

**GEORGE:**
But, Pop—

**JERRY** (thrusting him behind curtain):
If I hear one word out of you! If you even breathe heavy—

The door is flung open by the stage manager.

**STAGE MANAGER** (like a herald announcing a king):
Mr. E. F. Albee!

Albee strides in.

**ALBEE:**
I saw your show tonight, Cohan. Of course, it's no good for vaudeville but I've seen a lot worse—right here in Brooklyn.

28. **CLOSE SHOT    GEORGE**
He burns at Albee's words. He pushes the curtain aside to reply.

29.    FULL SHOT   DRESSING ROOM

Josie is standing right beside the curtain. As George flings it aside she promptly pulls it back into position, silencing George with a warning glance.

ALBEE:

> We're opening a new theater in Philadelphia—the Bijou—on the Fourth of July. If you can fix up a good vaudeville act, we'll double your present salary, give you a ten-week guarantee and third or fourth billing.

The Cohans look at him as if stunned for a moment. In their wildest dreams they have never dared hope for such excellent terms.

JERRY COHAN (dazedly):

> You'll double our salary!?

ALBEE (nods importantly):

> You'll be with the best variety stars in the country— (counts off on his fingers) Vosta Victoria, Eddie Foy, Ward and Vokes, Lottie Collins, Charlie Case—

Suddenly the curtain is pulled aside and George slips out.

GEORGE:

> Just a second. (To Albee, imperiously.) I'm George M. Cohan. You said you were opening a theater in Philadelphia on July fourth?

ALBEE (looking at him, curiously):

> That's right.

GEORGE (with an air of creating a sensation):

> That's my birthday.

ALBEE (dryly):

> That isn't why we're opening the theater.

The family pantomime pleading and threatening gestures to George, but he goes on.

GEORGE:

> The salary is all right, but how've you got the nerve to stick us way down in third or fourth billing— after *my* performance tonight?

His family stare at him in horror and panic. Albee removes the cigar from his moustache and gives George a slow once-over, as if trying to place him.

ALBEE (sarcastically):

> Is this kid in your show?

George's eyes pop wide in astonishment and indignation.

GEORGE (shouting):

> Am I in the SHOW! Who do you think was PECK'S BAD BOY!![21]

There is an awful moment of paralyzing embarrassment as all eyes fix on George, and his father's face looks like a thunderstorm just ready to break. Albee tries to avoid a family scene and smiles politely at George.

ALBEE:

> I beg your pardon. I didn't quite recognize you.

GEORGE (exploding):

> You didn't! Then maybe you're not the showman you're cracked up to be!

JERRY, NELLIE, JOSIE (together):

> GEORGE!!

ALBEE:

> Maybe I'm not. And maybe you're not ready for the big time yet. (To Jerry, Nellie, and Josie.) Good night.

He walks out.

30.    EXT. DOOR
As Albee opens the door  a crowd of actors who have
been eavesdropping quickly disperse.

31.    INT. COHANS' DRESSING ROOM
Jerry wheels on Nellie.

JERRY:
    See what we get because *you* wouldn't lay a hand
    on him all these years!?

NELLIE (nervously):
    A mother isn't supposed to do the punishing. She's
    just supposed to give her permission.

JERRY (looks balefully at George, then at Nellie):
    All right. Have I your permission?

NELLIE (with conviction):
    You certainly have!

Jerry advances on George, who retreats. Josie begins to
cry.

GEORGE:
    Pop—don't you think you ought to get my permis-
    sion, too?

Jerry grabs him by the hand, is about to rap him sharply
over the knuckles.

NELLIE:
    Not on the hand, Jerry. He's—he's got to play the
    violin.

JERRY:
    All right, not on the hand—

He lifts his hand to hit George on the mouth.

NELLIE (crying out):
    Not on the mouth, Jerry. He's got to sing!

112

Jerry looks at her, frustrated. Then, he sits down, turns George over on his lap.

JERRY (raising his hand to strike, as he looks at George's posterior):
This is one place without any talent!

Justice is taking its course, as we FADE OUT.

FADE IN

32.   MONTAGE   (WITH INSERTS)
Over a dark screen we SUPERIMPOSE the brightly lighted signs above theaters, flashing in various sizes which increase in importance, and often simultaneously in different corners of the screen, as we follow the Four Cohans through the dynamic decade that followed *Peck's Bad Boy*. This montage is scored throughout with such typical music of the period as "Ta-Ra-Ra-Boom-Dee-Ay," "Down Went McGinty," "My Mother Was a Lady," "In the Baggage Coach Ahead," and other golden ballads of the glittering nineties. INTERCUT with these are several old-fashioned pictorial billboards showing The Four Cohans. The SUPERIMPOSED TITLES read, in rapid succession:

KEITH & ALBEE'S BIJOU

ZIPP'S CASINO

THE CLEVELAND HIPPODROME

THE FOUR COHANS
in
*The Jester*

ORPHEUM THEATER—SAN FRANCISCO

*The Wise Guy*
with
THE FOUR COHANS

OVER THESE TITLES we bring Cohan's voice with a tone of affectionate reminiscence, as the QUICK SHOTS of the lithographed billboards show the Cohan family in various costumes and poses.

COHAN'S VOICE:
> The next ten years rushed by like a circus train, crowded with shows of every kind under the sun—and we played every town in America that had a theater . . . Millions of people came to know the Four Cohans as a sort of family tonic, taken year after year—just for fun. But in all those ten years—because I had gummed up the works with Albee—we had never played New York. Pop seemed content with the sticks, but I was straining at the leash. We were playing stock in Buffalo ... Being versatile, I was playing my mother's *father*—[22]

> SLOW DISSOLVE TO:

33.    SCENE ON STAGE    NELLIE
Nellie is sitting on the floor, her head on George's lap. We do not see George's face.

NELLIE (sobbing);
> Oh, Daddy, I loved him so! I loved him so!

33A.    CLOSE SHOT    MARY    IN AUDIENCE
She is a young, attractive girl. She watches the proceedings on the stage with the rapt attention of a stagestruck girl.

33B.    STAGE
We see Nellie, but not George. He speaks and the voice is old and quavery.

GEORGE'S VOICE (off-scene):
> The road to happiness, my daughter, is paved with heartaches and stones.

As he speaks the CAMERA PANS UP to his face. He wears a corny, foot-long divided beard and his hair is powdered gray. His forehead is covered with painted-on wrinkles.

The curtain comes down to terrific applause from an off-scene audience. When the curtain goes up, Georgie and Nellie are taking bows. Josie enters on curtain for specialty.

DISSOLVE TO:

34.  INT GEORGE'S DRESSING ROOM

The door opens and George comes in, followed by Tommy, a page boy.

TOMMY (at door):
Oh, George—there's a young lady—one of those stagestruck kids—would like to talk to you—

GEORGE (impatiently):
All right. Show her in. I'll make quick work of her.

Tommy, grinning broadly, opens the door. There stands Mary, a very nervous young lady. She is dressed in her Sunday best.

TOMMY (holding out his hand):
Mr. Cohan will see you, Mary.

MARY (effusively):
Oh, thank you.

She puts a coin into his outstretched hand.

TOMMY (with a wave of his hand):
He's all yours.

He beats it.

35.  MED. SHOT   MARY

as she steps diffidently into the dressing room. George looks at her inquiringly. She just looks back at him, too terrified to speak. George clears his throat, preparatory to breaking the silence, when suddenly Mary bursts out—

MARY (all in one breath and at a lightning speed, due to her nervousness):

> I'm eighteen—I sing and I dance and I'm going to New York, should I?

And having gotten this off her chest, she looks anxiously at George, who can only stare back at her very puzzled. Then,

MARY (so nervous she is close to tears):

> Oh, Mr. Cohan, you're so old, so experienced in the theater, so—so fatherly; do you think it's wise? I mean—my being eighteen—singing—dancing—going to New York?

George's eyes twinkle as he realizes she thinks he is really very old. He decides to keep on with the deception.

GEORGE (very fatherly):

> Well, my dear—your being eighteen, that's very wise. And so far as New York, the Four Cohans are going to break in there this fall.

MARY:

> Really? When are you leaving?

GEORGE:

> Right after tomorrow night's performance.

MARY (her face falling):

> I can't leave till Wednesday. I graduate from high school Tuesday.

The door opens and a very young, very pretty girl sticks her head in. She is a performer on the bill.

YOUNG GIRL:

> You haven't forgotten we have a date tonight, have you, Georgie?

GEORGE:

> I should say not. We're going roller-skating.

YOUNG GIRL:
>    Roller-skating? I should say not! There's a moon out! I'll be ready in five minutes.

She closes the door. Mary has been looking at George and the girl, shocked at this byplay—this doddering old man and this young slip of a girl.

GEORGE (to Mary, forgetting himself):
>    Pipperino, isn't she?

MARY:
>    Ye-es. Is she your daughter?

GEORGE:
>    Oh, I'm not married.

MARY (still shocked):
>    Then—your niece perhaps?

GEORGE:
>    No. Just a kid in the show. We've been datin'.

MARY (horrified):
>    Isn't she—isn't she a little young for you?

GEORGE:
>    Oh, no—she's all of seventeen.

Mary swallows her horror. After all, it's his life and his own business.

MARY:
>    Well—shall I sing for you? I know I have talent—even though I'm from Buffalo.

GEORGE:
>    Well, there's no piano handy—

MARY:
>    Then I'll dance.

She starts a buck-and-wing. Even for that day it is pretty corny. As she dances she looks anxiously at George for his opinion.

GEORGE (trying to be kind):

> It's—it's kind of old, isn't it? Everybody uses that step. You don't want to just imitate, do you?

MARY:

> Oh, no. Here's a step I made up myself.

And she goes into a dance which is really from hunger. George stops her gently.

GEORGE:

> On the other hand, you don't want to be *too* original, either— (She looks at him, crestfallen.) You just watch me a minute—I'll show you what I mean—

And he dances for her. It is a whirlwind dance that would tax the endurance of a boy of twenty. It is a strange sight, this bearded man, who looks eighty, nimbly performing these whirlwind capers.

MARY (looking at him in alarm):

> No! No!

GEORGE (still dancing):

> What's the matter? Don't you like it?

MARY (concerned):

> But so fast—such excitement—at your age— It can't be good for your heart— (Takes his arm, leads him to chair.) Please sit down and rest.

George, seeing her concern, decides to build it up.

GEORGE (sinking weakly into the chair, fingering his heart):

> Yes—perhaps I have—overdone it—a little.

Very casually he pulls her down on his lap. She thinks nothing of it. Such a tired old man.

MARY:

> My! Look at that perspiration on your brow—

She wipes his brow with her handkerchief. To her amazement the "wrinkles" on his brow come off on her handkerchief.

MARY (in amazement):
Your wrinkles! What happened to your wrinkles?

GEORGE:
Oh, I have to make up older than I am.

MARY (a little worried now):
How old are you?

GEORGE:
I can truthfully say that I am not yet seventy. (He gives her cheek a very fatherly pinch.)

MARY (relieved, but— ):
You seem different than when I first came in. Even your voice seems younger—

GEORGE:
I have a gift. I am as young as the people I'm with— (Pinching her cheek again.) You've made me feel very young again. Very young.

MARY:
I'm glad.

GEORGE:
Now! We'll make plans. Let's see—what managers shall I take you to see first? (Strokes the right side of his beard thoughtfully as he thinks.) Erlanger? Good old Abe— (Stroking the beard.) Maybe not right off— (Stroke.) Tony Pastor— Yes, that's better— (Stroke.) Albee? Koster and Bial? Poctor? (Stroke.)

By this time Mary is looking at him with intense horror.

MARY:
Oh!

GEORGE:
> What's the matter?

He follows her gaze to his right hand. The right portion of his beard has come off in his hand. While George looks at it, transfixed, Mary tugs at the remaining left portion of his beard. It comes off, as George howls "Ouch!"

Mary gazes a moment at the beardless youngster, then screams, jumps off his lap, rushes from the room. George looks after her regretfully.

GEORGE:
> If I were only twenty years older.[23]

FADE OUT

FADE IN

36.    CLOSE SHOT   A THEATRICAL BILLBOARD[24]
A large and brilliantly colored poster which reads:
HYDE AND BEHMAN'S
Special Labor Day Bill
Then there is a list of about five star acts. About halfway down the poster we see:
THE FOUR COHANS
in
"Goggles Doll House"

DISSOLVE TO:

37.    INT. THEATER   THE FOUR COHANS   ON STAGE
We see as much of their dance, "I Was Born in Virginia," as is desired. We note that it is going over very well with the audience.

38.    MARY   IN WINGS
dressed to go on. She is watching the Four Cohans intently—with special attention devoted to George. In back of Mary stands the manager—also giving his attention to the Cohans—and the audience's response is not lost upon him. He turns to his assistant.

MANAGER:

There's a contract on my desk—all typed. Bring it to me. And if any of the Four Cohans should ask you how you liked their act—say it's only fair.

39.   FULL SHOT   STAGE

The Four Cohans are exiting to loud applause. They pause at the side of the stage, and George gives his famous response to a good audience. Each one of the family responds in turn with a smiling bow or a curtsy.

GEORGE:

My mother thanks you—my father thanks you— my sister thanks you—and *I* thank you![25]

With a quick grin and a bow he disappears into the wings.

40.   BACKSTAGE

as the Four Cohans come off. They are surrounded by congratulatory actors.

ACTORS (ad lib):

Nice going, folks. That's tearing 'em out of their chairs. Hotter'n a pistol tonight, eh, George?

The Four Cohans smile, murmur their thanks; but George is busy looking around for Mary. As Nellie, Jerry, and Josie start for their dressing rooms they are hailed by the manager, who is doing his best to sound noncommittal and casual. George has spotted Mary and is off in her direction.

MANAGER:

Oh, Cohan—just a minute— (Walking toward them, contract in hand.) Not a bad act you've got there.

41.    MED. SHOT    GEORGE AND MARY
       in one of the wings.

MARY:

> You were wonderful, George! (Smiling.) But—I
> don't know—I miss that beard.

The orchestra strikes up a melody.

GEORGE:

> Thanks—but there goes the orchestra. You're on.

MARY:

> But George—that's not "Take Back Your Gold" . . .
> That's your song—the one we rehearsed all week.

GEORGE:

> Sure. I fixed it with the orchestra. Now all you've
> got to do is sing it.

MARY (worried):

> But the manager expects me to sing "Take Back
> Your Gold." You know what he says about changing
> an act . . . It's strictly forbidden.

GEORGE (contemptuously):

> "The manager says!" Who are they applauding out
> there—the manager or *me?* Now go ahead—

Mary looks out toward the stage, then grows pale.

MARY (quavering):

> Oh, George—I can't move—I can't go out there.
> It's—it's so different—from Buffalo!

GEORGE:

> What are you worried about? You're singing a
> George M. Cohan melody and a George M. Cohan
> lyric!

MARY:

> Ye-es, but it's my voice—

GEORGE:

—*discovered* by George M. Cohan! (Pats her shoulder.) Nobody ever had a better start . . . Lots of luck, kid!

He practically pushes her on.

42. STAGE

as Mary makes a somewhat ungraceful entrance, due to George's push. She is very nervous, but there is no hint of it in her singing as she begins the verse of the song. We stay on her as long as desired, then,

43. CLOSE SHOT   GEORGE   IN WINGS

listening with satisfaction to Mary's rendition of his song.

44. MARY   ON STAGE

singing with more confidence. She glances out of the corner of her eye to see if George is approving. When she sees that he is, she smiles delightedly.

45. BACKSTAGE   JERRY, NELLIE, JOSIE, AND THE MANAGER

Nellie, Jerry, and Josie look at each other hesitantly.

JERRY (to manager):

You see—it's this way. I'm speaking for the four of us. We decided we'd try our luck in New York and I don't think we'd want to go on the road again—in small time.

MANAGER:

Small time! You'd better read this contract. You play a full season in New York, and when you do go on the road it's the biggest houses in the biggest cities—Chicago, Philadelphia, Boston—!

The three Cohans stare at the manager in open-mouthed amazement. Josie reels a little.

MANAGER (has suddenly stopped as, for the first time, he realizes what is being sung on the stage):
> What's she singing? (Reaches into his pocket, comes up with a slip of paper, looks at it.) She's supposed to be singing "Take Back Your Gold"! Where does she come off—?! (To the Cohans.) Will you excuse me? Just get your makeup off—I'll be back in a minute.

He strides angrily away.

46.  WINGS  GEORGE
and a group of stagehands are gathered there. George's attention is centered on Mary. The manager strides into the scene.

MANAGER (to stagehand):
> Ring down the curtain on her!

George grabs the stagehand's arm as the latter is about to comply.

GEORGE:
> Wait a minute—be a sport—she's only got another eight bars to go—!

MANAGER (raging):
> Where does she come off—switching her song? We only put her on because the dog act got sick— (Whirling on George.) And come to think of it *you* recommended her!

GEORGE:
> She can put a song over, can't she?

MANAGER (suspicion growing):
> Say—I'm beginning to get a pretty good idea who poisoned those dogs—

GEORGE (defensively):
> They'll be as good as new by morning.

MANAGER:

Ah-*hah!* (To stagehand.) Ring down that curtain on her!

47.   MARY   ON STAGE
She bravely finishes the last of the song when *bang*—the curtain falls swiftly in front of her. Mary looks around, bewildered and anxious.

48.   FULL SHOT   AUDIENCE
a little mystified by the curtain's sudden fall, but showing their approval of the song and Mary by prolonged and enthusiastic applause.

49.   BACKSTAGE   GEORGE
is raging at the stage manager

GEORGE:

Ring that curtain up again! You can't pull the curtain down on a George M. Cohan song!

MANAGER (more light dawning):

Oh, so, in the bargain, it's your song! You wrote it!

GEORGE:

You can tell that by the applause. (Mary walks hesitantly into the scene.) Mary, I want you to go back for an encore—sing another chorus—milk 'em dry.

MANAGER:

You'll do nothing of the kind! (To assistant.) Get the next act on—*quick!*

A juggling act, two men and two women, rush onto the stage, glancing worriedly at the manager as they do so. The manager turns on Mary again.

MANAGER:

Young lady, you've sung your first and last song in vaudeville. If I were you I'd take my return ticket—

GEORGE (interrupting):

> Listen, knucklehead— If you've got any beefs un-
> load them on me! I'm the one that started this.

MANAGER (whirling on George):

> As for you, any more interfering and you'll be
> blacklisted in show business. You won't be able to
> get into a theater—your songs won't be able to get
> into a theater— (Mary, very close to tears, starts
> away.) Just a minute, young lady. I want the key to
> your dressing room— (Turns his back on George as
> he faces Mary.) The dogs are going back in in the
> morning!

This is all George can take. He lets go a roundhouse
kick that lands smack in the middle of the manager's
seat, sending him headlong against the backdrop,
which totters.

50.　　STAGE　THE JUGGLERS

are in the midst of a difficult feat. The curtain swings,
hits them—they and their props go flying as the backdrop comes down.

51.　　BACKSTAGE

All in confusion. The three Cohans have come out of
their dressing rooms. George, Mary by his side, is looking toward the fallen backdrop, in the folds of which
the manager is enmeshed—indeed, almost completely
hidden. Actors and stagehands are running around,
shouting, trying to rescue the manager.

52.　　CLOSE SHOT　FALLEN BACKDROP

It moves violently as the hidden manager tries to extri-
cate himself. Finally, his head comes into view. He is flat
on his stomach and speechless with rage. The first thing
his eyes fall upon is the contract lying on the ground
about two feet from him. He reaches out, snatches the

contract and—still lying flat on his stomach—tears it into bits.[26]

FADE OUT

FADE IN

53. EXT. DIETZ AND GOFF OFFICES DAY
CLOSE SHOT ENTRANCE DOOR (INSERT)
In an office building hallway the sign on a double door reads:

DIETZ & GOFF
THEATRICAL ENTERPRISES

DISSOLVE THROUGH TO:

54. INT. DIETZ AND GOFF'S RECEPTION ROOM TRUCKING SHOT
A busy theatrical office with three or four private rooms opening into the reception quarters. Through one of these private doorways comes the sound of a pianist banging out Cohan's "Harrigan," one of the first coon songs.

The CAMERA TRUCKS THROUGH THE RECEPTION ROOM past a group of show people who are waiting for interviews, reading theatrical papers, or talking to each other. The CAMERA HOLDS FOR A MOMENT on Sam Harris, also waiting. He is snappily dressed and is listening with interest to the lively piano music off-scene. As he turns slightly and looks toward the doorway, the CAMERA MOVES ON PAST HIM to a doorway marked:

SAM DIETZ
Private

Still MOVING TOWARD THE DOOR, the CAMERA

DISSOLVES THROUGH TO:

55. INT. DIETZ'S PRIVATE OFFICE FULL SHOT PANNING
A typical theatrical producer's office of the 1900s, its walls plastered with framed photographs of actors and actresses. George is seated at an upright piano, playing "Harrigan," and Mary stands close by, singing it to Goff and Dietz, two typical Broadway showmen of the pe-

riod, who are seated with cigars and blandly impassive faces. Mary is giving a swell job of selling the song and George comes in on the lines "Harrigan, that's me!"

MARY (singing):
 "Who is the man who will spend
 Or even lend?
 Harrigan, that's me!
 Who is your friend when you find
 That you will need a friend?
 Harrigan, that's me!
 For I'm just as proud of my name, you see,
 As an em-per-or, czar or king could be.
 Who is the man helps a man every time he can?
 Harrigan, that's me! "

GEORGE AND MARY (as they hit the refrain together):
 "H-A-double R-I-
 G-A-N spells Harrigan
 Proud of all the Irish blood that's in me,
 Divil a man can say a word agin' me!
 H-A-double R-I-
 G-A-N, you see,
 Is a name that a shame never has been
 Connected with,
 HARRIGAN, THAT'S ME! "

As they finish with a flourish, George and Mary look eagerly at the two producers.

GEORGE (eagerly):
 Well, what do you think?

GOFF:
 I didn't like it. Didn't appeal to me.

GEORGE (thunderstruck):
 Didn't appeal to—

DIETZ (to Goff):
 What do you mean it didn't appeal to you? (George

looks at Dietz hopefully.) I'm the senior partner around here. I make the decisions.

GOFF:
Well, what did you think?

DIETZ:
It didn't appeal to me either.

GEORGE:
Didn't like it! It's evident you gentlemen have no ear for music.

DIETZ (agreeing as he points to Goff):
*He's* got no ear for music. *I'm* the senior partner—I got a wonderful ear for music.

MARY:
But what about the libretto? It's a wonderful story, isn't it?

GOFF:
I laughed all the way through it.

DIETZ:
That's my cue. If Harold laughs then I know it isn't funny.

Goff nods in confirmation.

MARY (hastily, as George is about to explode):
Why don't you let Mr. Cohan sing the rest of the score for you? Maybe you didn't like "Harrigan" because I have no voice . . .

GOFF:
Oh, I think you have a lovely voice— (Quickly.) Don't *you*, Mr. Dietz?

DIETZ (to Mary):
Yes, you have a very nice voice. In fact, if you'd like a job answering our phone—

GEORGE:

> Just a minute! Are you or are you not going to pro-
> duce *Little Johnny Jones?*

DIETZ:

> If you think I'd put any of my wife's money into
> that trash, you're crazy.

GEORGE (exploding):

> That's enough, Mary! They've had their chance!

Angrily he starts to collect his music.

56.    OUTER OFFICE    SAM HARRIS
rises from his seat, walks to the receptionist's desk. He
has a script under his arm.

HARRIS:

> Do you think I can get in soon?

RECEPTIONIST:

> Have you an appointment?

HARRIS:

> Yes. My name's Sam Harris. I'm here to see them
> about a melodrama I own.

Just at this moment the door to the private office is flung
open. There is George, his back to the outer office, telling the partners off.

57.    MED. SHOT    GEORGE
Mary is at his side, trying to "shush" him.

GEORGE (pointing the finger of scorn):

> You don't know it yet, but you've had your day,
> boys. You're making way for the likes of me! (To
> Dietz.) Someday, Mr. Senior Partner, you're going
> to come to me and admit you were wrong![27]

DIETZ (grandly):

> In forty years in show business I have never once

admitted I was wrong— (Pointing to Goff.) That's his department.

GEORGE (not through with him yet):
   And as for your wife's money—!

But Sam Harris has come into the scene.

HARRIS (tapping George on the shoulder; quietly):
   Excuse me, please. I have an appointment.

And he goes into the private office, closing the door in George's face. George looks angrily at the closed door. The receptionist leaves to powder her nose. George and Mary are alone in the office.

MARY (trying to sound cheerful):
   Well, there's just enough time before dinner for us to see another manager.

GEORGE (dejectedly):
   Nope . . . This is the end of the list. We've seen them all.

Pause.

MARY (it's getting a little tough to be cheerful):
   Well, then, we'll start at the top of the list again. By now, they've had enough time to realize their mistake.

GEORGE:
   No—it's no use. (Pause.) Gosh, I hate to go back to that boarding house and tell the folks.

MARY (ruefully):
   You only have to go back to Forty-fifth Street. I have to go back to Buffalo.

GEORGE (intensely):
   No, you don't! They can keep throwing me out of offices—I'll keep coming back! I can write songs and plays faster than they can reject 'em. And once

I get one foot on Broadway, they'll never get me out again. And if you'll stay with me, you'll have your chance, too. You'll go right to the top with me![28]

Mary looks up at him. Her eyes are full of affection.

MARY (quietly, with a smile):
I never thought of leaving, George.

George moves closer to her, but at this moment voices are heard from the inner office and the door flies open. We hear Dietz's voice.

DIETZ'S VOICE:
Just a minute. I'm the senior partner. I do the throwing out!

HARRIS (backing out of the office, addressing Dietz and Goff):
That's the last time I'll ever offer you a play. (Quickly.) See you in the morning.

As he ducks he throws his hand up and a battered script comes flying into his hand. As Harris wheels around he bumps into George, almost upsetting him.

DISSOLVE TO:

57A.   DIETZ AND GOFF'S OFFICE   GEORGE AND MARY
as they emerge from Dietz and Goff's office.

MARY (self-reproachfully):
I spoiled everything. I was terrible—I was off-key.

George, who is burning up, catches sight of the receptionist, who is sitting calmly at her desk with rather a vacant stare on her face.

57B.   TRUCK SHOT   GEORGE
as he wrathfully makes his way to the receptionist's desk.

GEORGE (letting out his anger on the poor receptionist):
A fine pair of shoestring producers you work for! If

you had any self-respect you'd walk into their office and throw your resignation in their faces! Why, if I were you, I'd scrub floors. I'd dance in a saloon before I'd take a penny from those guys!

RECEPTIONIST (calmly):
    I practically don't. They owe me three weeks' salary now.

GEORGE (snatching up the phone in his anger):
    I'll call Klaw and Erlanger! They'll know a play when they see one!

RECEPTIONIST:
    No use trying the phone. They haven't paid the phone company either.

GEORGE:
    Why—

But he stops short as the sound of sniffling is heard off-scene.

57C.    MARY   ON BENCH   NEAR WATER COOLER
    She is trying to stifle sobs. George comes into the scene, sits down beside Mary.

GEORGE (sympathetically):
    Why—what's the matter, Mary?

MARY (tearfully):
    Buffalo—is—such— (sniff) a beautiful city. (Sniff.)

GEORGE:
    Is that what you're crying about?

MARY (still tearful):
    It's a beautiful city—but—but—I hate to go back to it.

GEORGE (with grim determination):
    Don't worry. You won't have to. I'll show them yet. I'll have all these sour-grape birds bowing and

scraping before long. I'll make this whole theatrical business sit up and holler for help, that's what I'll do. I'll show 'em! They'll all hear from me. Every one of them. They'll all hear from me!

57D.   MED. SHOT   RECEPTIONIST

RECEPTIONIST:
    You just raise your voice an octave and they'll hear you right now!

57E.   HARRIS
being thrown out of the office.

58.   EXT. A THEATRICAL BOARDINGHOUSE                NIGHT

59.   CLOSE SHOT   A SIGN NEAR DOORWAY   (INSERT)
Above the entrance a sign reads:
                    ROOM & BOARD
        Special Rates to the Theatrical Profession
                                    DISSOLVE THROUGH TO:

60.   INT. BOARDING HOUSE   DINING ROOM
with hallway and stairs visible in background.
    Madame Bartholdi, the boardinghouse keeper, is supervising the evening meal before she rings the bell for the boarders to "come and get it." Fanny, the waitress, brings in a heaping bowl of goulash.

MADAME BARTHOLDI (to Fanny):
    The juggler just paid three weeks' back board—put him at the center of the table so he doesn't have to reach for anything.

FANNY:
    Where shall I put the magician?

MADAME BARTHOLDI:
    Until he pays up, at the end of the table with the Cohans.

FANNY:

Oh, Starvation Corner.

Fanny starts to put the goulash a little too close to where the Cohans sit.

MADAME BARTHOLDI:

The goulash goes up at the other end of the table. I've told you that everything but the noodles and maple syrup is to be put out of the reach of the Cohans.

FANNY:

Noodles and syrup are just enough to keep 'em alive.

MADAME BARTHOLDI:

Anybody that owes me two months' board bill I just keep alive. I don't put weight on 'em.

During this conversation the five men and three women boarders, at the sound of the bell, have fairly bolted into the dining room and taken their regular seats. Jerry, Nellie, and Josie sort of trail in behind them and slip into their chairs. George's chair at the end of the table is empty. The magician and the juggler both go for the center seat at the table.

MADAME BARTHOLDI (giving a pleasant smile to the juggler):

From now on this is your seat . . . (Turning to magician with a cold stare.) And your seat is at the foot of the table with the Cohans.

MAGICIAN (glaring at her):

Some day I hope you will give me the pleasure of sawing you in half.

He goes to the designated seat at the end of the table.

All the boarders are spearing madly at the various dishes of food. The Cohans take sparse portions of noodles and sort of mince at them.

FIRST ACTOR:

> Just heard today Hammerstein is bringing over the Scotch actor Harry Lauder at twenty-five hundred bucks a week.

WOMAN BOARDER:

> Hammerstein's a smart showman . . . A lot of people have never seen a Scotchman.

Jerry Cohan timidly reaches for the bowl of goulash that is almost within his reach. Madame Bartholdi, seeing this, fairly swoops down on the bowl of goulash and starts serving the juggler, who is now the star boarder.

MADAME BARTHOLDI (to Jerry):

> Did you have that appointment with that gentleman this afternoon about your bookings?

JERRY:

> The appointment—oh yes—he's going to have some work for the act just any day now.

SECOND BOARDER (to Jerry):

> But I heard him offer you Boston.

JERRY:

> I didn't take the offer—it wasn't just right.

MADAME BARTHOLDI:

> Any act that's laid off as long as you have—*any* offer would be right.

Madame Bartholdi exits into the kitchen.

NELLIE:

> We just thought we'd rest a few more weeks.

JOSIE:

> George is writing us some new material. We're really not ready to open.

ANOTHER ACTOR (to Jerry):

> You're not fooling anybody, folks. Everybody knows

you and Nellie could get work tomorrow for the double and Josie's single, but nobody wants George.

61.  INT. BOARDINGHOUSE HALLWAY  FULL SHOT  GEORGE
He has entered from the street and is standing quietly in the hall, hanging up his hat. The open doorway to the dining room is close by and he has heard what was said. Already low in spirits because of his failure with the play, George's face tightens and he remains motionless while the CAMERA MOVES SLOWLY TOWARD HIS FACE.

SAME ACTOR'S VOICE:
You can't lay off the rest of your life because every manager in town has black-balled Georgie.

The CAMERA is now CLOSE ON Georgie's face as he listens, soberly, seeing himself as the failure of the family.

62.  DINING ROOM  FULL SHOT

NELLIE (spiritedly):
His family hasn't blackballed him. We may have to take a lot of hard knocks and make a lot of sacrifices, but if they want our act they'll have to take him too. We're not breaking up our act or our family.

JERRY (with even more spirit):
And let the blackballs fall where they may!

There is a moment of silence. George walks into the room as if he has heard none of the conversation, appearing breezily elated at something. Madame Bartholdi enters from the kitchen.

GEORGE (grandly):
Madame Bartholdi! Champagne for everybody!

MADAME BARTHOLDI (sarcastically):
Even if I had it, who would pay for it?

GEORGE:

> Dietz and Goff! They're putting on *Little Johnny Jones!*

There is a stunned moment as everyone stares at him excitedly.

NELLIE:

> George . . . Not really!

GEORGE:

> Yep. The book bowled 'em over and when Dietz heard the music he said the heck with his wife's money, he's gonna use his own!

JERRY (magnificently):

> The second round of champagne is on me! (To Madame Bartholdi.) *If* you had it.

JOSIE:

> Think of those billboards . . . Book—lyrics—music—all by George M. Cohan. Oh, George!

Then, characteristically, she starts to cry into her soup.

GEORGE (patting Josie on the shoulder):

> Take it easy, Josie—there's enough water in the soup already. (To Jerry.) Dad, I'll be all tied up in rehearsals the next few months, so I think you and Mom and Josie ought to take a job on the road to fill in.

NELLIE:

> That's a good idea. You get tired from resting too long.

The juggler is just lifting the dish of goulash to take another helping when Madame Bartholdi, with a cold stare, grabs it out of his hand, runs with it towards George.

63.    MED. CLOSE SHOT    MADAME BARTHOLDI AND GEORGE
She is overheaping George's plate.

MADAME BARTHOLDI (with a smile):
> If there's a part in your play for a bicycle rider, I
> used to be known as Venus on Wheels!

64.    FULL SHOT    BOARDINGHOUSE TABLE
Fanny and the actors take the cue from Madame Bartholdi and with lightninglike speed start pushing food
in the direction of the Cohans.

As the food passes the magician  he spears a carrot
off a plate and, opening his coat, feeds it surreptitiously
to a rabbit hidden inside.[29]

DISSOLVE TO:

65.    INT. RECTOR'S BAR                                    DAY
An establishing SHOT shows it to be a famous gathering
spot of show people of that period. There is a bar running almost the length of one side of the room. Near it
is a small group of tables. Directly across from the bar is
an alcove or small dining room. In it is a baby grand
piano, three gold bentwood chairs, and some artificial
palms.

Seated at one of the small tables we discover Sam
Harris and Schwab. Standing at the bar, within hearing
distance, is George Cohan. He is listening to their conversation. Harris and Schwab are unaware of this.

66.    MED. SHOT    HARRIS AND SCHWAB    WITH GEORGE IN
BACKGROUND

HARRIS (selling hard):
> When the villain says to the boy, "I'll tell the girl
> who you are unless you help me hold up the stage-
> coach . . . it's due in ten minutes . . . think fast,"
> you'll have the audience standing in their seats
> with excitement.

SCHWAB:
> So the hero helps him . . . gets shot in the leg and
> the girl nurses him back to health.

HARRIS:

It's not his leg, Mr. Schwab . . . it's his arm. And then what do you think happens next . . .

SCHWAB:

I won't be in the theater to find out. I'll be down the street watching a musical comedy. Before I put ten thousand dollars into a show it's got to have songs, dances, and a lot of girls.

HARRIS (undiscouraged):

Now the big scene is when the hero battles a forest fire to save the girl . . . It won't be expensive, Mr. Schwab, I know where I can get a cheap fire.

SCHWAB:

You don't need much of a fire . . . Just enough to burn that manuscript.

67.    MED. GROUP SHOT    FAVORING GEORGE
CAMERA PANS with George as he crosses to table where Harris and Schwab are seated.

GEORGE (to Harris):

Oh, here you are. Been looking all over for you. Come on—we've got to get going to Dietz and Goff's office and sign those papers.

HARRIS:

Wait a minute. What papers?

68.    MED. GROUP SHOT    GEORGE, HARRIS, AND SCHWAB

GEORGE (to Harris):

Oh, I see, you don't want to talk in front of Mr. Schwab. (Pretending sudden alarm.) Say, I hope you haven't discussed our *musical* with Mr. Schwab. You know what we promised Dietz and Goff . . .

HARRIS (still astounded):

Believe me—I haven't said a word about a musical.

GEORGE:

>    That's good. Dietz says it's the best musical he ever read, and he allowed Goff to agree with him!

HARRIS (still not wise; to George):

>    Just a minute, young fellow . . . Do you mind telling me—

George, realizing that Harris is about to give the whole thing away, quickly intercepts an approaching waiter.

GEORGE (to waiter):

>    Got the check for this table?

WAITER (handing it to him):

>    Yes, sir.

GEORGE (handing check to Schwab):

>    Glad to have met you, Mr. Schwab. (Practically pulling Harris out of his seat; to Harris.) Come on—we can't keep Dietz waiting.

SCHWAB (to Harris):

>    You're a fine guy. You've got girls up your sleeve and you don't tell me about it. What's it about?

GEORGE (quickly, to Schwab):

>    Haven't got time for details . . . It's about Tod Sloan in London. (To Harris.) Come on, partner.

HARRIS (finally catching on; addresses Schwab):

>    The famous jockey, you know.

Schwab's eyes light up. George and Harris stop and look at him hopefully.

SCHWAB:

>    Sounds swell. (Resignedly.) Just my luck to miss out on it. Well, good luck, boys.

He turns his attention again to his coffee.

69.   MED. CLOSE SHOT   GEORGE AND HARRIS

George looks disappointedly at Schwab, who has gotten off the hook, but he makes a quick recovery.

GEORGE (to Harris):
Oh, before we sign up with Dietz and Goff . . . I made a change in that "Yankee Doodle" lyric. I want you to hear it.

George starts to lead Harris toward the piano in the alcove.

HARRIS (playing it up; reprovingly):
You shouldn't have touched it. It was perfect the way it was.

70.   MED. SHOT   GEORGE, HARRIS, AND SCHWAB

SCHWAB (getting up from his chair):
Say—you don't mind if I just listen—

Immediately George and Harris each grab him by an arm.

GEORGE (as he practically drags Schwab toward the piano):
If you promise to be quiet.

DISSOLVE TO:

71.   ALCOVE OF RESTAURANT

George is at the piano, Schwab and Harris on either side of him.

GEORGE (singing):
"I'm a Yankee Doodle Dandy,
A Yankee Doodle do or die,
A real live nephew of my Uncle Sam
Born on the Fourth of July!
I've got a Yankee Doodle sweetheart,
She's my Yankee Doodle joy.

Yankee Doodle came to town
Just to ride the ponies.
I AM A YANKEE DOODLE BOY!"

SCHWAB:

I've heard enough! (To Harris.) I'll never forgive you for trying to palm off a forest fire on me when you had this musical all the time . . .

HARRIS:

But we gave our word to Dietz . . .

SCHWAB (angrily):

Why is Dietz's wife's money any better than my wife's money . . .? Must you give it to Dietz and Goff?

GEORGE (playing it up):

Well—I don't know. I like Dietz—but I don't think much of Goff.

HARRIS:

I'm crazy about Goff . . . I haven't got much use for Dietz.

SCHWAB (triumphantly):

See? You're in perfect agreement. I'll make out a check to bind the deal.

As he starts to write George and Harris wink at each other.

SCHWAB (as he writes; to Harris):

What's your partner's name?

HARRIS:

I don't know . . .

Schwab looks at him.

HARRIS (to George):

What *is* your name?

GEORGE:
> George M. Cohan. (Winking.) And what is my junior partner's name?

Schwab stares again.

HARRIS:
> Sam H. Harris. Shake.

They shake hands over the bewildered Schwab's head as the music of "Yankee Doodle Dandy" comes up strong.[30]

DISSOLVE TO:

72. INT. THEATER   CLOSE SHOT   A SLIDING TROMBONE IN ORCHESTRA
The trombone is blaring out "Yankee Doodle Dandy" with the rest of the orchestra, and from it the CAMERA PANS UP to:

73. FULL SHOT   THE STAGE ROUTINE OF "YANKEE DOODLE DANDY"
George is out front of the company on stage, wearing the sporty street clothes of the jockey and giving his famous rendition of "Yankee Doodle Dandy," singing and dancing. This routine of the hit number is given a good full production, INTERCUT from various angles of George and the ensemble. Also SHOTS of Mary in the chorus line, singing and dancing and watching George perform with much interest.

This can be held for two choruses of "Yankee Doodle Dandy," then the entire company swings into the big dance number. The audience gives a burst of thrilled, spontaneous applause.

74. CLOSE MOVING SHOT   WITH GEORGE AND MARY
As George dances back from the footlights and joins the rest of the company in the dance, he is next to Mary. The music and dancing continue at a fast tempo. He glances at her with appreciation as he dances past her.

75.   CLOSE MOVING SHOT   GEORGE AND MARY
Still dancing, George looks at Mary from the corners of
his eyes as if really seeing her for the first time. Mary
smiles back at him, flustered for a moment.

76.   FULL SHOT   THE STAGE
SHOOTING to include the first few rows of the audience.
The curtain begins to descend slowly on the still dancing company, and as it comes down the audience lets go
with a great and prolonged applause.

QUICK WIPE TO:

77.   FULL SHOT   BACKSTAGE   PANNING
Much hurried activity backstage during the scenery
change between acts, a general commotion of scene
shifters moving into action, orders being yelled to elec-
tricians and others, chorus girls running to make costume changes, etc. Grinning with elation, Sam Harris
comes up to George in the midst of the milling activity.
Outside the audience is still applauding.

HARRIS:
    It's a panic, George! Listen to 'em! We've got 'em
    eating out of our hands!

GEORGE (anxiously):
    I only hope the critics like it.

HARRIS (waves it aside):
    Who cares about the critics? We've got a SMASH.
    It's in the air, kid—it's in the air! (He slaps George
    on the back and gives the famous Harris slogan.)
    You can't stop anything that's in the air!

A callboy comes through, calling:

CALLBOY:
    Second act—places, everybody, please.

Sam Harris leaves and George departs in the direction
of his dressing room.

QUICK DISSOLVE TO:

78.   FULL SHOT   ON STAGE

The curtain is up on the last act, a night scene at a pier, with a gangplank leading up to a ship that is ready to sail. The chorus and other principals are going up the gangplank, chattering gaily and waving to friends on the pier. Down center of the stage George is standing with an older actor.[31]

79.   CLOSER SHOT   GEORGE AND THE OTHER ACTOR

The other actor leans close to George with a "confidential" stage whisper, loud enough for the audience.

ACTOR:

Now remember, Jones—watch for the skyrocket. If it goes off, you'll know that I've obtained certain papers from Anstey's cabin that will prove you innocent of throwing the English Derby. It will mean complete vindication. So stick here on the pier and watch for the skyrocket.

GEORGE:

Thanks, pal. (They shake hands.) I'll be watching.

CAMERA PULLS BACK FROM THEM AND PANS WITH THE OTHER ACTOR as he starts up the gangplank. The whistle blows on the ship.

JANE:

Good-bye, Johnny . . . and don't worry. *We* still believe in you.

The whistle on the ship blows again.

GEORGE:

That helps a lot, kid. Good-bye.

He kisses the real Mary, then realizing his mistake, kisses Jane. George runs down the gangplank. CAMERA MOVES to George's face as he looks after Mary. Orchestra begins "Give My Regards to Broadway."[32]

GEORGE:
> Yes—! (Begins to sing.)
> "Give my regards to Broadway,
> Remember me to Herald Square,
> Tell all the gang at Forty-second Street
> That I will soon be there—"

80.   FULL SHOT   STAGE   ROUTINE   "GIVE MY REGARDS TO BROADWAY"
George sings a verse and first chorus, then the entire company comes in on the second chorus as the ship begins to move away from the pier. A good fast song and dance routine to "Give My Regards to Broadway" follows with the chorus on the deck of the ship, INTERCUTTING from George on the pier to Mary on the ship, and to the full company.

81.   LONG SHOT   THE STAGE   HIGH ANGLE
for full effect of the "Give My Regards" number, at the end of which all on shipboard are waving and calling farewells to Little Johnny Jones on the pier, while the ship moves away.

QUICK WIPE TO:

82.   TRICK SHOT   ON STAGE
Little Johnny Jones is still on the dark pier, intently watching the ship, which by now appears to be far down the harbor in the moonlight, its tiny lights gleaming through the darkness of a moonlit night. Suddenly a rocket zooms up from the little ship in the distance, arches gracefully up into the top of the stage, and explodes like a brilliant scattering of stars. In the dark theater the effect is fascinating and thrilling.[33]

83.   CLOSE SHOT   GEORGE   ON STAGE
After giving the required reaction for the play, George cannot resist cutting his eyes toward the audience to see how the trick went over.

84.   QUICK SHOTS THROUGH THE AUDIENCE

They gasp in amazement and with wide eyes as they watch the extraordinary effect of the bursting rocket fade away. Then suddenly recovering their pose, they burst into enthusiastic applause, thrilled to the bone by Cohan's magic. The orchestra music swells up as the curtain rings down to a thunderous ovation from the audience.[34]

QUICK DISSOLVE TO:

85.   INT. MARY'S APARTMENT

Modest, but in good taste. Mary sits in an easy chair listening to George, who is pacing the room, reading from a manuscript.

GEORGE (reading):

"Then the train pulls out leaving Fred in the station. His uncle falls in the rain barrel. His aunt hides in the mailbag and gets mailed, special delivery to Cincinnati . . . A carload of chickens breaks loose and the hens are laying eggs all over the station as the curtain falls." That's the end of the first act. How do you like it?

MARY (enthusiastically):

It's even better and noisier than *Little Johnny Jones*.

GEORGE:

What do you think of your part so far?

MARY:

I like it because it's small. I'd be afraid to try anything bigger.

GEORGE:

Don't forget you've got something on the leading lady. You've got the best song in the show. Do you know it yet?

MARY (fervently):

I know every word right down to the copyright number.

She starts to sing "Mary." George sits down at the piano and accompanies her casually. As she sings she walks into the kitchen, tends to the things on the stove without missing a note. She is back in the living room for the finish.

GEORGE:
Even in the kitchen you sound like Tetrazzini.[35]

MARY (smiling):
In Buffalo they say I have—"a nice little voice."

GEORGE (contemptuously):
What do they know in Buffalo! (Smiles teasingly.) In Buffalo they thought I was an old man.

Mary smiles reminiscently.

MARY (sitting on the arm of George's chair):
You know—I never cared much for my name—kind of common—there are millions of Marys around—But now—

GEORGE (breaking in):
Listen. I didn't write that song for the millions of Marys. I wrote it for one particular, special Mary—

MARY:
It's a wonderful feeling—having your name set to music.

GEORGE (right in character):
And it isn't bad music, at that.

MARY (eyes aglow):
I want everybody to know that this song is my property, that it was written for me, that I'm *the* Mary—

GEORGE:
That's easy. On the sheet music, your picture on the cover—practically the same size as mine.

MARY:

> That won't do it— (Ruefully.) Because—darn it—I look like the millions of other Marys . . .

86. CLOSE SHOT  GEORGE
as he looks at Mary.

GEORGE (slowly):

> They'll know all right. When they look at you, singing that song—and they look at me, looking at you— (Pause.) They'll know. They'll know all right.

86A. MED. SHOT  MARY AND GEORGE
Mary looks at George affectionately.

MARY (gratefully):

> George—

GEORGE (interrupting):

> No. When you say "George," say it as if George were a grand old name too.

Pause.

MARY (with great affection):

> George—

Their heads are very close together when suddenly the doorbell rings. Then, without waiting for the bell to be answered, Sam Harris flings the door open.

86B. MED. SHOT  AT DOOR
as Harris comes in.

HARRIS (to George):

> I thought this is where I'd find you. Come on, we've got to get to the Lyceum before Fay Templeton goes on.

GEORGE (springing to his feet):

> Fay Templeton! What does she want to see us about?

HARRIS:

>She doesn't want to see us; we want to see her. Her play's closing. We'll offer her the lead in your new show.

GEORGE (awed):

>Fay Templeton! Do you think she'll take it?

HARRIS (hustling him toward door):

>Of course not. But it's a chance to see what she looks like without makeup.

86c.   MED. SHOT   AT DOOR

MARY (to Harris):

>What do you think? George has written a number for me to sing in the show!

GEORGE (his usual modesty):

>Not a number, *the* number.

MARY (to Harris, who has the door open):

>Do you think I'll be able to do it justice?

HARRIS:

>Why not? You've got a nice little voice.

Mary and George look at each other, then Mary good-naturedly pushes Harris out of the door.

>DISSOLVE TO:

87.   HUGE SIGN   OVER THEATER
which reads:

>ERLANGER AND KLAW
>Present
>FAY TEMPLETON
>in
>*A Little Bit of Everything*

A paste-on strip in one corner proclaims:

>"2nd Big Year"

And underneath:

>"Last Week"

>CAMERA PANS FROM SIGN TO:

88.  STREET  TRUCKING SHOT  GEORGE AND HARRIS
as they walk toward the stage door of the theater.

HARRIS:

> One thing in our favor, Erlanger is with us and he's got a lot of influence with Templeton.

GEORGE:

> All right, you devote your time to Erlanger—I'll tackle Templeton.

HARRIS (worried):

> Please, George, you don't "tackle" a star like Miss Templeton—you "approach" Miss Templeton. And very tactfully, too.

GEORGE:

> Well, if it's tact that does it—it's done.

They enter the stage door.

89.  BACKSTAGE
as George and Harris enter they see Dietz, dressed to kill, a huge bouquet of flowers in his hand, talking to the stage doorman.

DIETZ (to the doorman):

> If you'll see that I get in to Miss Templeton, I'll give you— (magnanimously) two passes for my next show.

HARRIS:

> Well, if it isn't Mr. Dietz.

GEORGE (to Dietz):

> You look naked without Goff. (Takes the flowers right out of his hand.) I'll see that Miss Templeton gets your flowers. (Removes one rose, hands it to Dietz.) My compliments to Mrs. Dietz. (To Harris, as they walk away.) How's that for tact?

Dietz stares after them.

90.    INT. FAY TEMPLETON'S DRESSING ROOM

A large, well-furnished dressing room that includes a small piano. Templeton, in the process of making up for her performance, is arguing with Abe Erlanger.

ERLANGER:
You've got to remember, Fay, that we're having a tough time lining up your next vehicle. You ought to listen to this man. He's just written a big hit.

TEMPLETON:
*One* hit. He may be a flash-in-the-pan for all we know. And I saw *Little Johnny Jones*. One act was all I could stand. Of all the loud, vulgar, flag-waving—I'm looking for a quiet, dignified musical play. I want to perform in a theater, not a boiler factory . . .

There is a knock on the door.

ERLANGER:
Come in.

91.    MED. SHOT    AT DOOR

as Harris and George come into the room.

ERLANGER:
Hello, Sam. How are you, Cohan?

Harris and George say hello.

ERLANGER:
Fay—may I present Mr. Harris?

TEMPLETON (matter-of-factly):
How do you do?

ERLANGER:
And Fay—this is Mr. Cohan—George M. Cohan.

Templeton barely nods in George's direction.

92.     CLOSE SHOT   GEORGE

He has decided to play the timid, bashful boy struck dumb by the sight of this beautiful, glamourous, temperamental creature.

GEORGE (all stops out):
    Miss Temp— (His voice sticks in his throat, his eyes go to the floor.) I—that is—I—

93.     FULL SHOT   ROOM   GEORGE

is still playing "Charles Ray." Harris looks at him, amused, knowing what he is trying to do. Templeton, on the other hand, is flattered by this display.

GEORGE (suddenly bursting forth):
    Oh, shucks, Miss Templeton— I've never been at a loss for words before—but—but—standing here in your presence— (Suddenly he thrusts the bouquet of flowers toward her like an awkward schoolboy.) Here—let these speak for me!

TEMPLETON (touched):
    Why, Mr. Cohan—how sweet.

She reaches for the flowers, but the effect is spoiled by the door suddenly bursting open to admit Dietz.

DIETZ (seizing the flowers):
    I'll present my own flowers, thank you. (Handing them to Templeton; reverently.) Miss Templeton, may I have the honor of drinking champagne from your slipper tonight?

Before the astonished Templeton can answer, Harris has shoved Dietz out of the door.

HARRIS (closing the door on him):
    Goff's the junior partner. He does the drinking.

As Templeton stares, still astonished, George, not the least perturbed, takes the flowers out of her arms.

GEORGE ("reverently"):
> Miss Templeton, may I have the honor of putting these flowers in water for you?

Erlanger suppresses a smile. Templeton sits down before her dressing table.

TEMPLETON (not knowing whether to be angry or not):
> Well, really. I—

She picks up her slipper to put on her foot.

94.     MED. SHOT   GEORGE
as he puts the flowers in a vase, he takes a look at the slipper. Its size is not altogether dainty.

GEORGE (in a stage whisper, to Harris):
> If that's the slipper he's going to drink out of, he's going to have quite a jag on in the morning.

HARRIS:
> Sssh!

95.     FULL SHOT   ROOM   TEMPLETON
has heard, or thinks she has.

TEMPLETON (getting to her feet; sharply):
> *Mister* Cohan—!

HARRIS (quickly):
> Well, shall we get down to business?

TEMPLETON:
> There's really no use discussing anything. (To George.) I'm afraid I would never please the sort of people who revel in your antics and fireworks.

GEORGE:
> You're just modest, Miss Templeton. I bet if you let yourself go you could be just as noisy and entertaining as the rest of us. You might even have some fun yourself.

Templeton turns her back on George, addresses Erlanger.

TEMPLETON:
Abe, isn't it time for the curtain to go up?

HARRIS (pleading):
If we could have a few minutes of your time after the show—

TEMPLETON:
I'm sorry. After the show I'm going right home to New Rochelle. It's only forty-five minutes from here, but thank heavens it's a thousand miles from all the noisy, neurotic people one has to associate with in our profession.[36]

And with a pointed look at George, she sweeps out of the dressing room, followed by Erlanger.

ERLANGER (soothingly):
Now, Fay—

The door closes behind them. Harris turns on George.

HARRIS:
That tact of yours! That wonderful tact!

GEORGE (not even listening to Harris; musingly):
Forty-five minutes from Broadway—

DISSOLVE TO:

96. WINGS

SHOOTING OUT toward stage. We see the curtain coming down. Erlanger is standing in the wings, waiting for Templeton to come off. He rushes to meet her.

ERLANGER:
Have you thought it over, Fay?

FAY:
I'm not interested in Mr. Cohan or his plays.

She starts for her dressing room.

97.    TRUCKING SHOT    TEMPLETON AND ERLANGER
as they make for her dressing room.

ERLANGER (earnestly):
You're making a mistake, Fay. He's the most original thing that's ever hit Broadway. And do you
know why? (Templeton shrugs indifferently.) Because he's the whole darn country, squeezed into
one pair of pants! His writing—his songs—even
the way he walks and talks—they all touch something way down *here* in people! (He lays a hand
over his heart.) Don't ask me why it is—but it happens every time the curtain goes up. It's pure
magic![37]

They are ascending the stairs now to her dressing room.

TEMPLETON:
I'm bored by magic. I know his formula—a fresh
young sprout gets rich between 8:30 and 11:00 P.M.

ERLANGER:
That's just it! George M. Cohan has invented the
success story, Fay. And every American loves it because it happens to be his own private dream. He's
found the mainspring in the Yankee clock—ambi-
tion, pride, and patriotism. That's why they call
him the Yankee Doodle Boy.

They are outside her dressing room now.

ERLANGER:
If you'll take my tip, Fay, you'll do what I'm going
to do—hitch your wagon to his star—right now.

TEMPLETON (dismissing the subject):
I've got to change for the second act, Abe— (She
tries to open the dressing room door; it doesn't
come open.) Who locked my door?

She tries again; it still won't open. From inside the
dressing room comes the sound of a piano.

TEMPLETON (knocking on the door):
>  What's happening here?

The door is opened from the inside, Harris sticks his head out.

HARRIS:
>  Sssh! He'll be through in a minute.

He closes the door. Templeton and Erlanger look at each other in amazement. Then the door opens again. Harris appears.

HARRIS (apologetically):
>  Oh, excuse me—I didn't realize it was you. Come right in.

98.  INT. DRESSING ROOM   GEORGE
who is at the piano, gets up as Templeton and Erlanger come into the room.

GEORGE (waving a piece of paper):
>  It's all finished! (To Fay.) And you gave me the inspiration!

TEMPLETON (puzzled and annoyed):
>  Do you mind telling me—

GEORGE:
>  When you said you lived forty-five minutes from Broadway the idea hit me. The perfect title for my show—and what an idea for a song! Here it is, Miss Templeton—dedicated to you.

TEMPLETON:
>  You mean to say that while I was on the stage just for one act you wrote an entire song?

GEORGE (grinning):
>  I was working in strange surroundings—that's what took me so long.

ERLANGER:
> He worked so hard, Fay. The least you can do is
> listen to it.

TEMPLETON:
> All right. (Steps behind a screen.) I'll dress here.

99.  GEORGE
as he rushes to the piano, starts "Forty-five Minutes
from Broadway." During the song we CUT TO REACTION
SHOTS of the others. Templeton, despite herself, is impressed.
> When the song is finished, Harris, in his enthusiasm,
steps behind the screen.

HARRIS (stepping back hastily):
> Oh, excuse me— Look, Miss Templeton, that's just
> a chorus number. But he's got one song—"Mary"—
> that's just perfect for you . . .

GEORGE (in sudden alarm):
> Hey—! (Pulling at Harris's coattails.) Not "Mary"—
> she doesn't sing that!

HARRIS (waving him aside; to Templeton):
> Wait till you hear it— It's the best thing he's ever
> done!

GEORGE:
> No! She won't like it—it's just a so-so number—

TEMPLETON (stepping from behind the screen):
> If it's as good as "Forty-five Minutes from Broad-
> way"—

GEORGE:
> It isn't! And besides—

The door opens; the callboy sticks his head in.

CALLBOY:
> Curtain going up for second act.

TEMPLETON (to Erlanger):
> You handle all the details, Abe. I may have been wrong about Mr. Cohan.

GEORGE (frantically):
> But, Miss Templeton—

But she is already out of the dressing room.

GEORGE (desperately to Harris):
> Ge-ho-sophat! How'm I going to tell Mary about this!

HARRIS (expansively):
> That tact of yours, George. That wonderful tact![38]

DISSOLVE TO:

100.    HALLWAY    OUTSIDE MARY'S APARTMENT
George, staggering under the load of a huge bouquet of flowers and a tremendous box of candy, comes into the scene. He is about to ring the doorbell when, from inside the apartment, he hears Mary playing "Mary" on the piano. George winces, but rings the doorbell. After a moment the door is opened by Mary.

MARY (looking at the flowers and candy):
> A little early for Christmas, isn't it?

101.    INT. APARTMENT
as George steps in.

GEORGE (casually):
> Oh, I just happened to be passing the florists. They threw in the candy.

MARY:
> George—I'm sure our song will live forever. I've been playing it ever since you left and the neighbors haven't complained once.

George laughs—but uneasily.

MARY (eagerly):
>What happened with Fay Templeton?

George sits down at the piano, casually picks out the notes of the score—this while he fishes for a way to break the news.

GEORGE:
>Oh, she's dying to play the part; but—I don't know—I haven't made up my mind yet—[39]

MARY (amazed):
>You mean you're hesitating about having Fay Templeton in your show?

GEORGE:
>We-ell—you know how these big stars are—temperamental—lay down a lot of terms and conditions—

MARY:
>I think you ought to give in to her.

GEORGE:
>No matter what she asks?

MARY (firmly):
>No matter what she asks.

GEORGE:
>Say, why are you so concerned for Templeton?

MARY (earnestly):
>I don't care for Templeton. I'm looking out for you. Think what it means for you to have a star like Templeton in your second show!

George looks at her.

GEORGE:
>Always worrying about me, aren't you? Don't you ever think about yourself?

MARY (looking at George steadily):
> Haven't had time. The minute I saw you without your beard I knew here was a little boy who would need a lot of looking after— (Pause.) I gave myself that job. There are a lot of singers, but only a few really good looker-afters.

GEORGE (he takes both her hands into his and his heart is in his eyes):
> Listen, darling—how would you like to make it a lifetime job? Leading lady—no options. There may be a little heartache in the show at times, but I'll guarantee you a million laughs, too . . . How does it sound?

MARY (starry-eyed):
> I think I might like it, Mr. Cohan. Could I see some of the script?

GEORGE (beaming):
> Well, here's how it starts—

He takes her into his arms and kisses her.

102.   CLOSE TWO SHOT   FAVORING GEORGE
as they hold each other tight, then slowly a troubled look crosses George's face, the terrible dread of complete confession.

GEORGE:
> Honey—there's just one little thing I forgot to tell you.

MARY (softly):
> Yes, George?

GEORGE (takes a deep breath, then the dive):
> I—I gave your song to Fay Templeton tonight.

He holds his breath, waiting for the storm to break.

103.  CLOSE TWO SHOT   FAVORING MARY
Still in his arms, she smiles slowly, a Mona Lisa smile.

MARY (quietly):
> I knew you did, dear—when you brought the candy and flowers.

On George's bewildered take, we

SLOW DISSOLVE TO:

104.  EXT. NEW AMSTERDAM THEATER   NEW YORK   NIGHT
FULL SHOT   MARQUEE
The huge electric sign above the New Amsterdam theater entrance emblazons to the world:

COHAN & HARRIS PRESENT
FAY TEMPLETON
in
GEORGE M. COHAN'S NEW
MUSICAL COMEDY HIT
*Forty-five Minutes from Broadway*

The gay and lively music of the theme song comes out strongly over this shot. (If story and production value warrant the point we might show or indicate the smart New York crowds that jammed the theater throughout the run of this smash hit, and the SRO sign which stayed out for months.)

DISSOLVE THROUGH TO:

105.  INT. THEATER ROUTINE   FORTY-FIVE MINUTES FROM
BROADWAY
NOTE: This has been shot.[40]

DISSOLVE TO:

106.  CLOSE SHOT   FAY TEMPLETON   ON STAGE   LONG DOLLY
(NOTE: This has been shot.) Fay Templeton looks radiantly beautiful as she sings with much feeling and charm through the first verse of "Mary's a Grand Old Name"; then into the lovely refrain as the CAMERA BEGINS TO PULL BACK from her. She smiles tenderly toward one of the boxes.

FAY TEMPLETON (singing):
"For it is Mary, Mary,
Plain as any name can be,
But with propriety, society
Will say Marie—
But it was Mary, Mary,
Long before the fashion came,
And there is something there
That sounds so square—
It's a grand old name!"

The curtain comes down to great applause from the audience.

107.  MED. THREE SHOT  IN BOX  GEORGE, MARY, SAM HARRIS
George is sitting with Mary, and Sam Harris is sitting in the semi-darkness behind them. Both men are wearing full dress and Mary is in a lovely gown of the period with big puff sleeves and the "Gibson Girl" hairdo. George is holding Mary's hand gently on the arm of her chair, and they both look very happy. The applause continues.

After a moment Sam Harris leans forward and pats George on the shoulder in a close, friendly gesture.

SAM HARRIS:
That's a great song, George—the best you've ever done. It'll live for years.

GEORGE (turns and smiles gratefully):
Thanks, Sam— (he looks at Mary, as if still not sure that he's squared) but I still think Mary should've had it.

The CAMERA MOVES UP CLOSER to them now as Mary smiles at George tenderly and shakes her head.

MARY:
It's all right. Fay has the song—I've got the author.

She looks down at her hand. CAMERA FOLLOWS her gaze
to the wedding ring on her finger.

DISSOLVE TO:

108.   LONG SHOT   STAGE   SLOW DOLLY TOWARD TEMPLETON
(NOTE: This has been shot.) In another stage setting for
the final act Fay Templeton is singing richly and tenderly the other great hit number from the show. The
rest of the company is behind her in background.

FAY TEMPLETON (singing):
   "So long, Mary,
   Mary, we will miss you so . . .
   So long, Mary,
   How we hate to see you go.
   We'll all be longing for you, Mary,
   While you roam . . . "

The CAMERA is now CLOSER to her and she looks up with
a smile of affection toward the box where Mary, George,
and Harris are sitting as she concludes the song.

FAY (continuing):
   "So long, Mary—
   Don't forget to come back home."[41]

FADE OUT

FADE IN

109.   INT. WAITING ROOM   RAILROAD STATION         NIGHT
A small waiting room of a middlewestern railroad station. Jerry, Nellie, and Josie are waiting for a train to
take them to their next engagement. The telegraph operator is closed off from the waiting room in a glass-
partitioned office. Seated in the background are two
young actresses surrounded by a violin case, a banjo
case, a piano-accordion, and their personal baggage.
They are sound asleep. Seated next to them is another
actor reading a newspaper. Jerry is standing, looking
through the window into the darkness. A driving rain
hits against the glass. He goes over to the old-fashioned
stove, opens its door, takes the coal scuttle, and pitches

some coal into the dying fire. Nellie is knitting and Josie has turned up her suitcase and is using it as a writing desk. She is busily engaged writing a letter.

110. MED. SHOT

Jerry, after putting coal on fire, looks at his hands smeared with coal dust disgustedly.

JERRY (to Nellie):
> There isn't one waiting room in the Midwest that has a clean coal scuttle. Remind me to write a letter to the railroad authorities.

NELLIE (still knitting):
> You've been writing that letter for twenty years, but I'll remind you.

JOSIE (looking up from her letter writing):
> Is it the robin that tells us it's the first breath of spring?

JERRY:
> How can you think of robins in the spring when we're freezing to death in the Middle West?

The actor with the newspaper suddenly looks up.

ACTOR (handing Jerry the newspaper):
> Look at the way they're billing you in Waukegan.

JERRY (reading):
> "Jerry, Josie, and Nellie Cohan, the family of George M. Cohan, the new Broadway sensation . . ."

NELLIE (hastily, before Jerry can explode):
> Well, that's true. He *is* the biggest thing on Broadway!

JERRY (breaking out):
> No, sir! We built our reputation and we do a good act, and they'll bill us as the Three Cohans like we should be billed!

NELLIE (soothingly):
> All right. All right. No need to excite yourself.

JERRY (to actor):
> I don't want you to get the idea I'm jealous of George's success—even though I'm a better dancer.

ACTOR (smiling):
> Of course you're not jealous.

NELLIE (proudly):
> There'll be no stopping George. All he needs is a little more experience and he'll be a genius.

JERRY:
> We must never let him know that I'm the better dancer. It might interfere with his becoming a genius.

ACTOR:
> Still—it does seem a little funny—George being the toast of Broadway and you folks just picking up crumbs in the tank towns.

Jerry and Nellie look at each other uncomfortably. The telegraph operator slides a little glass panel and calls out:

TELEGRAPH OPERATOR:
> Which one of you folks is Jerry Cohan?

JERRY:
> I am.

Jerry walks over and takes telegram and reads it, a broad smile on his face, then reads it aloud to Josie and Nellie and the actor.

JERRY:
> It's from George. "Impossible to find three clever actors named Cohan for my new show anywhere in New York. Return immediately for rehearsals."

NELLIE (excitedly):

> Josie, did you hear that? The Four Cohans back together and on Broadway!

ACTOR (enviously):

> Look, can't you make me a member of the family? I'm half Irish.

The train whistle is heard. The two sleeping actresses arouse themselves, start getting their baggage together. The other actor grabs his suitcase; the Cohans prepare to leave the waiting room.

Josie folds her letter. It consists of about twelve sheets of paper.

JOSIE:

> And I'm just getting started on this letter.

As they start out  Jerry trips over the coal scuttle, falls on his face.

JERRY (to Nellie, from the floor):

> Remind me to write in about that coal scuttle.

As train whistle comes over again,

DISSOLVE TO:

111.  LARGE SIGN OVER THEATER

COHAN & HARRIS PRESENT
THE FOUR COHANS
in
*George Washington, Junior*
starring the author-composer
GEORGE M. COHAN

OVER THIS SHOT comes the music of "The Grand Old Flag."

DISSOLVE THROUGH SIGN AND ZOOM UP TO:

112.  INT. THEATER   FULL SHOT   THE FOUR COHANS   ON STAGE

Back together, Jerry, Nellie, Josie, and George are dancing and singing to "The Grand Old Flag," while the chorus line dances behind them in background. The happiness on the Cohans' faces as they work together and smile at each other is something to see.

THE FOUR COHANS (singing as they dance):
> "There's a feeling comes a-stealing
> And it sets my brain a-reeling,
> When I'm listening to the music of a
>     military band!
> Any tune like 'Yankee Doodle'
> Simply sets me off my noodle,
> It's that patriotic something that
> no one can understand!"[42]

113.     INTERCUTS  ROUTINE OF "GRAND OLD FLAG"  ON STAGE
As they hit the chorus with rousing effect, George produces the flag. We INTERCUT the number from the Four Cohans to Mary, dancing in the chorus and watching George with much affection, and also to Sam Harris watching from the wings.

COMPANY TOGETHER (singing and dancing):
> "You're a grand old flag,
> You're a high-flying flag,
> And forever in peace may you wave.
> You're the emblem of the land I love,
> The home of the free and the brave!
> Every heart beats true
> Under red, white, and blue,
> Where there's never a boast or brag—"

On this next line we give a QUICK CUT to the Four Cohans as they smile at each other with shining eyes.

> "But should auld acquaintance be forgot—"

Then a FLASH SHOT of Mary, who sees the Four Cohans' look and understands it, her eyes also shining.

> "Keep your eye on the grand old flag!"

114.   FULL SHOT   THE STAGE
As George and the entire company swing into a fast ensemble dance number we CUT AROUND to the audience
for its enthusiastic applause. Cohan and Harris have
done it again.

SLOW DISSOLVE TO:

115.   MONTAGE   ROAD TOUR   "GEORGE WASHINGTON, JR."
A fast series of overlapping DISSOLVES cover the triumphal tour of the Cohan and Harris smash hit. Against
long STOCK SHOTS of Boston, Chicago, St. Louis, Philadelphia, and San Francisco we SUPERIMPOSE FLASH TI-
TLES of the cities' names. These are INTERCUT WITH
QUICK SHOTS of trains, the show on various stages, and
CUTS of the cast riding in pullmans, singing and laughing. The effect is one of hectic movement, success, and
gaiety: the "Great Golden Age" of the American theater,
when "the road" was a fabulous gold mine and show
business was a warm human adventure. Music from the
hit numbers of the show underscores the montage
throughout.[43]

Following this is a series of titles of more of George
M. Cohan's hit shows. Over this montage we SUPERIM-
POSE the years: 1906, 1907, 1908, 1909, 1910, 1911, 1912,
1913, 1914, 1915.

DISSOLVE TO:

116.   COUNTRY HOUSE
on a knoll, overlooking a vast expanse of rolling hills.
The CAMERA TAKES IN the beauty of the place, then,

CUT TO:

117.   BARBECUE PIT   ON LAWN
Nellie Cohan and Mary are setting six places on a tablecloth that is spread over the lawn. A few feet away Jerry
Cohan and Sam Harris are trying to get a fire going in
the barbecue pit. Even at this distance we can see that
they are very inexpert at it. A cow ambles into the
scene, steps on the tablecloth.

NELLIE:

Shoo! Get away from here, Little Johnny Jones—

"Little Johnny Jones" obediently turns and ambles away.

MARY (enviously):

My, what authority you have with cows! And you a farmer only three weeks.

NELLIE:

It's hard to believe that till I met Little Johnny Jones the only cows I'd ever seen were from a train window. (Looks toward Jerry and Harris.) Jerry is still scared of the creatures.

118.    MED. SHOT    JERRY AND HARRIS

puttering around the fire. No flame is yet to be seen.

JERRY (disgustedly):

I should have played with matches more when I was a kid, then maybe I'd be able to start a fire now.

Smoke shoots up from the pit.

HARRIS (encouraging):

Well, we've got smoke. Fire can't be far behind.

JERRY:

When George and Josie get in with the wood I'll really show you something— (Looks cautiously in the direction of the women.) This is very humiliatin'—especially on my birthday.

119.    MED. SHOT    GEORGE AND JOSIE

Both are breaking twigs off trees. George is doing a good job, but Josie's mind appears to be on something else. After a moment she breaks the silence.

JOSIE:

George—what did you get Dad for his birthday?

GEORGE:
Nothing.

JOSIE:
Nothing?

GEORGE (very casual):
Practically nothing. I just wrote him a letter.

JOSIE:
What kind of a birthday present is that?

GEORGE (carelessly):
Well, my signature should be worth something.

JOSIE:
It's going to look awfully silly up against what I got
Dad. (Reaches into her pocket.) Look at this.

She hands a watch case to George. He opens it and dan-
gles a beautiful gold watch.

GEORGE (impressed):
Wow! Tiffany's!

JOSIE (proudly):
With an engraved sentiment. That cost extra.

GEORGE:
Where did you get the money for this?

JOSIE:
Oh, I don't have to pay for ninety days— (Hesitates, steels herself, then says casually.) But I'll be
married by then—I'll borrow the money from my
husband.

George looks at her, astounded.

GEORGE:
You'll be *what* by *when?*

JOSIE (feeling better now that the leap has been taken):
Married—as soon as Fred's road tour is over.[44]

George is silent as the realization sinks in. Then,

GEORGE (slowly):
> It's hard to realize— Doesn't seem so long ago— Mom and Pop on the road— You and me in school in Syracuse—

JOSIE:
> You were ten, I was seven.

GEORGE (suddenly):
> Josie? What does this do to the Four Cohans?

JOSIE (just as affected as George is, but trying not to show it):
> Oh, just a simple case of subtraction. One from four leaves the Three Cohans.

GEORGE:
> Do Mom and Pop know?

JOSIE (nodding):
> Mom's been working on the wedding dress for weeks—

George is silent, lost in thought.

JOSIE (gently):
> What are you thinking about, George?

George looks at her, smiles.

GEORGE:
> I've got an idea for the best goldarn wedding march that was ever written— (Looks at her, scratches his head.) Say, are you sure I'm only three years older than you are?

Josie smiles, kisses George affectionately.[45]

DISSOLVE TO:

120.    FULL SHOT    GROUP    AROUND FIRE
Jerry Cohan is the center of attraction. He has a pile of

gifts in front of him and is going through them. He holds up the watch Josie has given him for all to see.

JERRY:

> It's a very beautiful watch, but— (kidding around, he takes out his battered Ingersoll and compares its time with Josie's watch) it's three minutes fast.

Everyone laughs.

GEORGE:

> Dad—will you tell Josie that just because she's getting married is no reason to break up our act? The Four Cohans is just as sacred an institution as marriage.

Jerry clears his throat.

JERRY:

> I'm afraid, George, that your mother and I are breaking up the Four Cohans before Josie is.

George looks at him.

GEORGE (incredulously):

> You're just saying that. Wait till you read the part I've written for you in my next play. It's almost as good as my part.

MARY:

> And wait till you hear the songs.

NELLIE (to George):

> It's been a forty-year run, remember. All I ask now is to be allowed to spend the rest of my days on this beautiful farm.

GEORGE:

> You can't put an actor out to graze, Mother. The fresh air kills 'em. (To Jerry.) There can't be just *one* Cohan on Broadway!

JERRY:

With you writing, acting, producing, directing, singing, and dancing the public will think there are a hundred Cohans on Broadway.

Pause.

GEORGE:

Dad—are you really serious about this retiring business?

JERRY:

Any actor giving up applause is no joking matter. You'll find that out.

GEORGE:

Well, then—I think it's time you read my birthday present.

JERRY:

I will—as soon as I get my glasses on. (He takes out an old pair of spectacles from a case.) It's a wonder no one thought of a new pair of glasses for a birthday present. I should have been more definite in my hints. (He has the letter open now.)

GEORGE (pointing to the fire):
Step up front to the footlights, Dad.

JERRY (doing so):
I'll indicate when I want applause. (Starts to read.) "Dear Dad: This is your birthday and God bless you. Maybe I've never told you before but no one has ever had a better dad or one to be prouder of—"

Everyone has become very quiet. Jerry stops for a moment, looks over the rim of his glasses at George.

JERRY (back to the letter):
"You and mother have always given me more love and understanding than I ever deserved, and all

the luck I've had is due to the things you've taught me. Nothing I can do could ever begin to repay that debt and I know you don't expect it, Dad, but here's a little present for you and Mother—"

Jerry stops, affected.

NELLIE (also affected, but trying to help Jerry out):
Why me? It's not my birthday.

JERRY (reading again):
"To begin with, I deed to you this farmhouse and everything in it. From this day on you and I are partners in every theater and theatrical property I possess, one half and equal. The Cohan theater, the theater in Chicago for which we broke ground last week—and in all my plays and songs, as long as they or you and I will live—"

Jerry has become more and more affected, his voice lower and lower. Finally he can go no farther.

JERRY (taking off his glasses):
Those aren't my reading glasses—I'd better not go on—

George takes the letter from his hand.

GEORGE:
There isn't much more—just— (reading very earnestly) "With all my love, your son and partner, George."[46]

Nobody speaks. All eyes are on Jerry and Nellie. Jerry makes a tremendous effort to control himself. Now he is ready to speak.

JERRY (with much emotion):
George—George—on behalf of your mother and myself—

This is as far as he gets, for Nellie suddenly bursts into tears.

JERRY (turning on Nellie):
You would steal this scene from me with an obvious piece of business!

Everyone laughs, breaking the tension.[47]

FADE OUT

FADE IN
121.   EXT. THEATER
Two bill poster men are engaged in putting up a huge bill poster on the side of the theater. Other workmen are busy getting the outside of the theater in shape for what is evidently opening night. When the bill poster is finally up we see that it reads:

COHAN AND HARRIS
Present
GEORGE M. COHAN'S BRILLIANT DRAMA
*Popularity*
With an all-star cast

Over this activity George's voice is heard:

GEORGE'S VOICE:
One success followed another. We built another theater. But there was one challenge I hadn't met. People who were envious of my success—and Broadway was full of 'em—said that musicals and cheap comedies were all I could write. I could wave a flag, they said, and nothing else. I was determined to show 'em. I wrote a legitimate drama—no music, no flag waving. *Popularity* it was called—and no opening was so important to me. I *had* to show Broadway—and myself. The night *Popularity* opened I was playing in *The Yankee Prince* and couldn't attend—but my mind wasn't on my own performance—[48]

DISSOLVE TO:

122.   BACKSTAGE THEATER
Loud applause is heard offstage. George exits from the

stage in his *Yankee Prince* costume. His manner is very preoccupied. He makes for his dressing room. The stage manager accosts him.

STAGE MANAGER (with some surprise):
> Oh, Mr. Cohan—you're not going to your dressing room, are you? You're good for another five curtain calls.

GEORGE:
> Let the curtain stay down. It's enough for tonight.

123. TRUCK SHOT   GEORGE AND STAGE MANAGER
as they walk toward dressing room.

STAGE MANAGER (anxiously):
> Mr. Cohan—are you sure you're feeling well?

GEORGE (tersely):
> I'm all right—any word from *Popularity* yet?

STAGE MANAGER (looking at his watch):
> Nope. They should be ringing down just about now.

GEORGE (irritably):
> You'd think Sam or my folks would have run over between acts and let me know what's happening.

He goes into dressing room.

STAGE MANAGER (as he follows him in):
> That's a good sign. They're too engrossed in the play.

124. INT. GEORGE'S DRESSING ROOM

STAGE MANAGER:
> I've got the reports here from Detroit on your minstrel show. Rave notices again.

GEORGE (getting out of his costume):
Rave notices—that's bad. How much did it lose on the week?

STAGE MANAGER:
Ten thousand, more or less.

GEORGE (shaking his head):
The better the notices you get on minstrel shows these days, the more you lose. What's our total loss so far?

STAGE MANAGER:
Just a few dollars under two hundred thousand.

GEORGE (ruefully):
Is that counting the cost of the red ink? Boy—*Popularity* better be a hit tonight. We've got plenty sunk in that too. Not to mention my ego.

STAGE MANAGER (dryly):
Oh, everybody mentions your ego.

GEORGE (not ill-naturedly):
Get out of here, wise guy, and turn out the footlights. We've got to start saving money.

As the stage manager starts out  the door opens to reveal Sam Harris, Mary and Jerry and Nellie Cohan. They are a pretty solemn-looking lot. The stage manager looks at them, and they look back at the stage manager without saying a word. The stage manager nods understandingly and slips by them. George, in the meantime, has been waiting impatiently.

GEORGE:
All right—speak up—yes or no—which is it?

Nobody speaks. Finally Mary blurts out.

MARY (loyally):
I loved every minute of it! I don't care what the others thought!

NELLIE (backing her up):
> The ending of the second act was the funniest—I laughed myself sick and so did the rest of the audience!

GEORGE (ruefully):
> But, Mom, the end of the second act is very dramatic. You weren't supposed to laugh.

NELLIE (crestfallen):
> Oh.

JERRY (right from the shoulder):
> No use beating about the bush, son. It was ghastly.

HARRIS (gloomily):
> It wasn't that good.

JERRY:
> The smartest thing to do is forget it— Everybody's entitled to *one* mistake. (He smiles and holds out his hand.) Now come on and let's have our party— just as if the show was a hit.

The CAMERA PANS to favor George as all of them look at him. He is still too dazed by his failure to react normally.

GEORGE:
> Yeah—sure—sure, we'll have the party. (Pauses, looking at them.) Dad, you and Forrest take the girls on over to Delmonico's. (Looks at Harris.) Sam and I'll join you in half an hour.

With uncertain glances and not yet sure why George hasn't exploded, the others agree to the suggestion and withdraw from the dressing room.

DISSOLVE TO:

125.　EXT. BROADWAY SIDEWALK　(PROCESS)　　　NIGHT
MED. FULL TRUCK SHOT　GEORGE AND HARRIS
They are walking through the crowds on the sidewalk, wearing dark hats and topcoats over their dinner

clothes. George still looks fighting mad and Harris deeply concerned. The noise and traffic of Broadway continues throughout the scene.

GEORGE (angrily, inspired):
Listen—we'll put an ad in all the papers—"*Popularity*, the biggest smash hit in town! Seats sold out ten weeks in advance!"

HARRIS (alarmed):
Hold on, kid—you can't do that!

GEORGE (belligerently):
Why can't I?

HARRIS:
Because I don't want you to! (Earnestly.) It wouldn't be on the level, George. We've got too big a reputation to try and fool the public by plugging a flop. They'd never forgive us for it.

GEORGE (snaps back sulkily):
Don't keep calling it a "flop," will you? I don't like that word!

HARRIS:
Okay—I'll call it anything you say—except a hit.

They walk on in silence for a few steps, through the hurrying Broadway throngs. Finally Harris glances at George and smiles.

HARRIS:
Come on—stick your chin out, kid. Show 'em you can take it.

George cuts an eye at him but says nothing, walking on, as the CAMERA CONTINUES TO PULL BACK WITH THEM. But he is thinking now, calming down. His eyes become shrewd.

GEORGE (suddenly):
You're right, Sam—everybody in New York will be

waiting tomorrow to see if I can take a licking. They'd love to see me squawk—yell murder—pull a crybaby act. That's just what they *expect* from me . . . (He pauses in front of a Western Union office, turns to Harris with a gleam of sly excitement.) But I'm going to pull a twist on 'em! Come on in here!

He grabs Harris's arm and hustles him into the telegraph office.

QUICK DISSOLVE TO:

126.  INT. THE TELEGRAPH OFFICE
George and Harris are standing at the counter. George rips off the top sheet of the pad and hands it to Harris.

GEORGE:
I want to wire this ad for tomorrow to every paper you can catch. Here's the copy . . .

Harris takes the paper, looks puzzledly at George, then reads what George has written.

HARRIS (reading):
"To the theater-going public of New York City: I humbly apologize and beg forgiveness for writing and producing so poor a play as *Popularity*—Last five performances—PLEASE MISS IT—George M. Cohan."[49]

Harris laughs with enthusiasm and George smiles, tosses a bill on the counter, and they walk out of the telegraph office.

127.  EXT. SIDEWALK  BROADWAY  TRUCK SHOT       NIGHT
As George and Harris emerge onto the sidewalk from the telegraph office and start to walk, an excited newsboy suddenly rushes past, waving an "extra" and shouting:

NEWSBOY:
Extra—*Lusitania* sunk without warning!—Over one thousand killed!

George and Harris stop, as do others on the sidewalk, staring after the newsboy. Farther down the street other boys take up the cry.

GEORGE (in a subdued tone):
 And here's me thinking the failure or success of a show was important.

All down the crowded, brightly lighted street newsboys are running and yelling the startling story to excited crowds.

NEWSBOYS:
 *Lusitania* sunk by German U-boat! Twelve hundred lost on *Lusitania!* 124 Americans killed, including 75 women and children!

QUICK FLASHES OF GROUPS eagerly scanning the newspapers on the sidewalks, of George and Harris poring over a copy with grim-set faces. Underneath these shots begins the angry roar of an enraged people, building in volume and tempo. The scoring is fast and exciting, like a storm approaching and ready to burst. Now around the electric news-band of the Times Building at Forty-second Street runs the blazing news item:
 GERMANY PROCLAIMS
 UNRESTRICTED SUBMARINE
 WARFARE . . . THREATENS U.S.A.
 IN SHARP NOTE . . .

  DISSOLVE THROUGH TO:

128. NEWSPAPER HEADLINES (INSERT)   MONTAGE EFFECT[50]
 ZOOMING UP over STOCK SHOTS of huge American crowds in city streets, come newspapers with bold headlines:
 UNITED STATES DECLARES WAR ON GERMANY!

129. FULL SHOT   EXT. ARMY BUILDING   WHITEHALL
 STREET                                        DAY
 A sign reads:
  U.S. ARMY RECRUITING OFFICE

A brass band is playing as a come-on, and already a long line of volunteers in civilian clothes is waiting to get in. A couple of recruiting officers are strutting around, soliciting trade. It is a gay, noisy, typical 1917 scene.

WIPE TO:

130.  INT. EXAMINATION ROOM   PANNING
The band music outside continues through this scene. A half dozen recruits are stripped to the waist and undergoing examinations by army doctors, while recruiting sergeants assist, hurrying the men along. Among the volunteers is George, also stripped to the waist and barefooted. He looks very eager and patriotic. The CAMERA MOVES UP to him and an army doctor who is inspecting his feet. After a moment the doctor lets George's foot drop, looks up, and shakes his head.

ARMY DOCTOR:
No—sorry, but we can't use you, Mister.

GEORGE (amazed as the doctor turns away):
Hey, what's wrong with me!?

DOCTOR:
You've got flat feet. In fact, two of them.

131.  CLOSE-UP   GEORGE
He stares at the doctor a second, then explodes with righteous indignation.

GEORGE:
WHAT! *Me?* The best hoofer in show business! You're crazy!

132.  FULL SHOT   GROUP
As the other recruits and soldiers look toward George he points to them excitedly, making quite a scene.

GEORGE:
I'll walk against *any* of these guys—from the Bat-

tery clear up to the Bronx—and guarantee to beat
'em by three miles! Whaddya mean "flat-feet"?
Why, I can—

Suddenly an army sergeant, a big burly fellow, comes
up behind the irate, arguing George, half lifts him by
his belt, and starts away with him.

SERGEANT (kindly but firm):
Listen, buddy—we're trying to get an army together—so move on, will ya? (He takes George's
shirt off a peg and tosses it to him.) Here's your
shirt—compliments of Uncle Sam.

The other recruits and soldiers laugh at George's
flushed face, as mumbling darkly, he pulls on his shirt.

WIPE TO:

133.  OMITTED

134.  EXT. ARMY BUILDING   TRUCK SHOT   GEORGE
As George comes out, looking very dejected at being
turned down, the recruits still waiting in line look at
him without recognition. One of them, a big truck
driver, grins sympathetically and calls out to him.

TRUCK DRIVER:
Tough luck, pal—but don't worry—*we'll* take care
of 'em over there![51]

THE CAMERA MOVES with George's face as he walks by
the line of men, with a smiling glance toward the well-
wisher. Then after a few steps further he suddenly gets
a thoughtful look. In background the brass band is still
playing.

GEORGE (quietly, tasting the words):
. . . over there . . .

In the background a bugler with the brass band slips
out and blows a military call on the bugle. The first
three notes are very similar to what is later to be the

opening three notes of "Over There." George is struck by these three notes. He walks to the bugler.

GEORGE (to the bugler):
Do you mind repeating that?

BUGLER (blankly):
What?

GEORGE:
*That*. Da-da-*da!*

BUGLER:
Oh that! Sure.

He blows the military call again.

GEORGE:
Louder!

The bugler looks at George out of the corner of his eyes, but complies.

DISSOLVE TO:

135.    MONTAGE
of TRICK SHOTS of bugles, all blowing these thematic three notes. From a CLOSE SHOT of a bugle,

DISSOLVE TO:

135A.    CLOSE SHOT    BUGLE
being blown by Sam Harris. The CAMERA PULLS BACK TO REVEAL the scene as George's office. George is in his shirt-sleeves working hard with one hand and jotting down the notes of the new song with the other. At the same time he keeps motioning to the very livid Sam Harris to keep blowing on the bugle.

GEORGE (worriedly):
"Over there . . . over there,
Send the word, send the word . . . "

135B.   CLOSE SHOT   GEORGE'S HANDS
as he plays the notes.

LAP DISSOLVE TO:

136.   CLOSE SHOT   MUSICAL INSTRUMENTS   PANNING   NIGHT
CAMERA STARTS on two pianos, side by side, with four
hands at the keyboards, playing. All around them are
other instruments of a complete orchestra, all playing
"Over There." CAMERA PANS UP to George at one of the
pianos. It is still impossible to tell just where this scene
is. Then slowly THE CAMERA PANS UP from George to the
platform, draped in American flags. Fay Templeton,
beautifully dressed, is singing.[52]

FAY TEMPLETON (sings with orchestra accompanying):
"Over there, over there—
Send the word, send the word, over there,
That the Yanks are coming,
The Yanks are coming!"

137.   LONG SHOT   ENTIRE SCENE   INT. AN ARMY
CANTEEN                                       NIGHT
The platform upon which Fay Templeton is singing is in
the center of an army camp, and it is surrounded by a
crowd of American soldiers, listening tensely to the
new song being heard now for the first time anywhere.

GEORGE (to Templeton):
Let's go, Fay. (To the soldiers.) Everybody together!

With a roar of eager applause the soldiers' voices join
Templeton's in a surging choral effect. Clearly George's
song is an instantaneous hit.

TEMPLETON AND SOLDIERS (singing):
"Over there, over there,
Send the word, send the word, over there
That the Yanks are coming!
The Yanks are coming!
The drums tum-tumming everywhere!

So beware, so beware!
Send the word, send the word to beware!
We'll be over,
We're coming over
AND WE WON'T COME BACK
TILL IT'S OVER OVER THERE!"

DISSOLVE THROUGH TO:

138. MONTAGE "OVER THERE"
This fast montage should be the most exciting and colorful part of the entire picture and wants a careful routining for highest effects. Behind all the scenes there continues a strong chorus of male voices singing "Over There" in a marching, military manner.

1. SHOTS of U.S. soldiers marching and singing "Over There."[53]

2. Bands playing it everywhere, and orchestras, individuals, people of all ages and types—a nation united with one great song.

3. Army camps—thousands of tents and barracks—swarms of soldiers. Naval bases, shipyards with the workers riveting on ships and singing "Over There."

4. Army parade down Fifth Avenue, N.Y.—the regiments in war packs, infantry, artillery, cavalry, leaving for France.

5. Soldiers marching up gangplanks to the transports, all singing. Cheering thousands are seeing them off, the women with tear-dimmed eyes, calling out, "Good-bye—good luck!"

6. The convoyed transports at sea.

7. A flash shot of N.Y. paper with the headline:
CONGRESS CALLS COHAN'S "OVER THERE"
THE AMERICAN HYMN OF VICTORY!
Composer Congratulated by President Wilson

8. War shots—the fighting in France, battle scenes.

9. Inserts of newspaper headlines:
ARMISTICE DECLARED!
GERMANY DEFEATED!

10. Parade up Fifth Avenue, N.Y., of the returning and victorious American troops.

11. TRUCKING SHOT of George—in the parade, still the irrepressible kid who loved a parade, the bands, the flags. He marches along beside the soldiers with other civilians, proud and happy, carrying a small flag over his shoulder.

FADE OUT

FADE IN

139.  EXT. BROADWAY    LONG SHOT    PANNING        NIGHT
OVER A NIGHT SHOT of Broadway's theatrical district, flashing with innumerable signs of new shows, theaters, we hear on the sound track a fast medley of "Jazz Age" music; then,

COMMENTATOR'S VOICE:
Nineteen hundred and twenty—"The Roaring Twenties!"—Broadway is ablaze with lights and life and music— in the sensational boom of show business that followed the war! America wanted to laugh and sing and dance—and one man spoke for all—George M. Cohan![54]

140.  LONG TRICK DOLLY SHOT    DOWN BROADWAY    WITH MONTAGE EFFECTS
The CAMERA IS MOVING CONTINUOUSLY THROUGHOUT THIS SHOT as if down the crowded center of Broadway. As it passes the many brilliantly lighted theaters we HOLD briefly on the electric signs to show the famous run of Cohan and Harris hits that followed the war. This movement is fast but on each title we SUPERIMPOSE the year and HOLD long enough for a snatch of the hit music from each show. The effect is of a great continuous medley, perhaps with voices singing the lyrics of the best-loved numbers.

One after another on the theater fronts we read beneath the line "Cohan and Harris present":

1919: *The Royal Vagabond* . . . 1920: *Mary* with its great Harbach-Hirsch song "Just a Love Nest" . . . 1921: *The O'Brien Girl* . . . 1922: *Little Nellie Kelly* with "Nellie Kelly, I Love You" and "You Remind Me of My Mother" . . . George M. Cohan in *The Song and Dance Man* . . . "I Guess I'll Have to Telegraph My Baby" . . . 1927: *The Merry Malones* with the great hits "Easter Sunday Parade" and "Blue Skies, Gray Skies" . . . *Billie* with "Where Were You, Where Was I?" and "Billie" . . . 1931: *The Tavern* . . .

And finally, 1934: "The Theatre Guild Presents George M. Cohan in *Ah, Wilderness!* by Eugene O'Neill."

DISSOLVE TO:

141.    EXT. COHAN FARMHOUSE        NIGHT

There is a light burning in an upstairs window. A dim light is also visible in a hall.

DISSOLVE TO:

142.    UPSTAIRS HALL   IN FARMHOUSE      NIGHT

The hall is empty. Then the bedroom door opens and two doctors and a nurse come out. Their expressions are very grave.

FIRST DOCTOR (to nurse):

> Give him two more ccs. We might as well try to make him as comfortable as possible.

NURSE:

> Yes, Dr. Anderson.

She goes back into the bedroom, closes the door quietly behind her. The doctors speak in hushed tones.

DR. ANDERSON (to his colleague):

> If you have to get back to town, Dr. Llewellyn—I'll be here all night—

DR. LLEWELLYN:

> That's all right. I'll wait till George M. gets here from the theater.

Dr. Anderson nods, opens a cigarette case, offers one to Dr. Llewellyn.

DR. LLEWELLYN:
Thanks. (Lights cigarette; musingly.) I remember I was a kid in medical school when I saw the Four Cohans. They were a great act.

DR. ANDERSON (nodding):
I always thought George M.'s sister was the loveliest dancer I had ever seen.

DR. LLEWELLYN (looking toward the bedroom):
I can't help thinking—a theatrical era is dying in there. The sister and mother gone—now the old man— In some ways I think he was the best performer of the lot . . .

DR. ANDERSON:
Well, I'll settle for his age— There was nothing dull about his life, either. And he's lived to see his son an American institution. I'd settle for that, too.

The door is heard opening and closing downstairs. Then the sound of footsteps on the stairs. In a moment George, followed by Mary and Sam Harris, comes into the scene.

GEORGE (anxiously):
Doctor—

DR. ANDERSON:
Hello, Mr. Cohan.

DR. LLEWELLYN (to George):
I think you'd better go in alone.

The doctor's tone tells George the bad news. His face sets, then quickly he goes to the bedroom door, opens it, and goes in.

143.    INT. BEDROOM

as George comes in. The nurse, who has been sitting by the bedside, gets up, nods understandingly to George, then tiptoes out of the room. George looks anxiously and lovingly at his father.

144.    CLOSE SHOT   JERRY

The tossing of his head and the mumblings of his lips tell us that the first faint stages of delirium have set in. George comes into the scene.

GEORGE:
> Pop—

Jerry looks at him with glazed eyes.

JERRY (half making sense, half in delirium):
> Oh, here you are—where you been? Not every kid gets a chance at Peck's Bad Boy— Are you nervous? Do you know your lines?

His cover has slipped down.

GEORGE (fixing the cover):
> Sure I do. I can lick any kid in town.

JERRY (same as before):
> Good boy—if you upstage your mother I'll beat the livin' tar out of you— Nellie— You hit him—I'll hold him—

He leans his head against his pillow, exhausted. George smooths the cover.

JERRY (his eyes opening again):
> Madame Bartholdi—champagne for everyone— Book, lyrics, songs, dances—everything by my son, George—No sir, we've always been billed as the Four Cohans and we're not splitting up the act—(He is silent a moment, then.) Stop it! Stop it, Nellie— Don't steal my scene with an obvious piece of business!

Jerry shows signs of becoming excited.

GEORGE (soothingly):
    Take it easy, Pop.

145.    CLOSE SHOT    JERRY
    He relaxes, his eyes closed. When, after a moment, he
    opens them again it is plain that for the moment he is
    lucid.

    JERRY (feebly, in greeting):
        George—

146.    MED. SHOT    JERRY AND GEORGE

    JERRY:
        How—how did it go tonight?

    GEORGE:
        Fine. Six curtain calls.

    JERRY:
        Six—not bad for a drama.

    Silence.

    JERRY (eyes a trifle glazed again):
        Did you—did you thank them for all of us?

    GEORGE:
        I sure did— (Trying to keep his voice steady.) "My
        mother thanks you—my father thanks you—my
        sister thanks you—and (voice breaking slightly) I
        thank you."

147.    CLOSE SHOT    JERRY
    He smiles faintly. His eyes close. His expression is
    peaceful.[55]

148.    HALL    MARY, HARRIS, AND THE DOCTORS
    They stand about silently. All heads turn quickly toward
    the bedroom as the door opens slowly. George comes

out. His expression tells the story. Mary goes to him quickly, puts her arms around him.

DISSOLVE TO:

149. INSERT    FRONT PAGE OF "VARIETY"

The bible of show business carries in bold headlines, and with their pictures, the biggest theatrical news story of the year:

BOMBSHELL HITS BROADWAY!
COHAN AND HARRIS PART COMPANY!
Famous Partnership Dissolved
After Decades of Sensationally
Successful Play Producing

DISSOLVE TO:

150. INSERT    CLOSE SHOT    A BLOTTER

The blotter carries the firm name Cohan & Harris Theatrical Producers, with one half carrying a picture of George and the other half one of Harris. Slowly a man's hands tear the blotter into exact halves.

CAMERA PULLS BACK TO:

151. INT. COHAN & HARRIS OFFICE    MED. TWO SHOT    AT DESK

George and Harris are sitting casually on the edge of a large desk in Harris's private office. George takes the half-blotter with his picture and hands it to Harris, then takes the half with Harris's picture and tucks it into his wallet. Then they smile at each other with the deep understanding of two old friends. There is a note of regret and kindly affection in their voices.

GEORGE (nods to the half-blotter):
    It was a great firm, Sam.

HARRIS:
    Yep. Now that it's all over—who was the senior partner and who was the junior partner?

GEORGE (smiling):
    You mean—who was Dietz and who was Goff?

(Harris nods smilingly.) Well, I guess we were the only one combine in existence with *two* senior partners. (Pause.) You understand, don't you? About my leaving—

HARRIS:
Sure—I don't blame you a bit.

GEORGE:
When Pop died that was the last link to the Four Cohans. There just doesn't seem to be anybody to play to anymore. The old thrills, the applause, the backslapping—somehow, they don't seem important anymore. Not with Dad, Mom, and Josie gone. Mary and I are going to travel—have some fun— forget we ever saw a theater—meet people who never even heard of me.

HARRIS:
You'll have to go to Timbuctoo.

GEORGE:
As a matter of fact, it's on the tour. (Sticking out his hand.) Good-bye, Sam.

HARRIS (taking his hand; earnestly):
You're the one with the words, George. I don't know how to say things— We did more than just make a lot of money together—and now and then, lose a little— We were partners, but friends. Lots of times people drift apart— Let's not let it happen to us, George.

GEORGE:
Sam—I don't care how legally our partnership is dissolved—fifty percent of me will always be here— in this office.

HARRIS (smiling faintly):
Thanks. I'll remember that when the rent comes due.

GEORGE:

> I know you're going to be a greater success than
> ever, Sam, but—if the rent ever does come due and
> you can't meet it—

He looks steadily at Harris.

HARRIS (trying not to show how much he is affected):

> Okay. I'll wire you collect in Timbuctoo. Now, get
> out of here before that old boat sails without you.

Arm in arm, they go into the anteroom.

152.  ANTEROOM

The room is buzzing with reporters in a great state of
excitement. They are besieging the girl at the reception
desk. We hear: "We've got to see them." "I know they
had a fight. It's all over town!" "Then why is Cohan
sailing for Europe?" But they stop short, and all the conversation dies as they see George and Harris come into
the room arm in arm.

REPORTERS AD LIB:

> What's this? We thought you guys weren't speak-
> ing to each other. Can we have a picture of you and
> Mr. Harris tearing up your contract?

HARRIS:

> That's impossible. We never had a written contract.

GEORGE (taking Harris's hand and shaking it):

> This is the only contract we ever had.

REPORTER (snapping photograph):

> Hold that pose. We want to show it to our legal
> department.

The several photographers crowd up to snap the shot
with flashes, but George and Sam are still looking at
each other. As they smile and the flashing lights continue

DISSOLVE TO:

152A.   MONTAGE SHOTS
showing George and Mary on the various stages of their trip around the world. London, Paris, Cairo, Buenos Aires, etc.[56]

DISSOLVE TO

152B.   ORCHARD   GEORGE
a few years older now, is stretched out on a hammock reading a copy of *Variety*. A jalopy pulls up bearing two couples of high school age. A column of steam is erupting from the radiator.

BOY (calling to George):
Hey, Mister— (George looks up.) Our radiator needs some water. Can we use your well?

GEORGE:
Sure. Help yourself.

They pile out of the car, make for the well.

GEORGE (to one of the boys as he goes past):
What's wrong with your radiator?

BOY:
Varicose veins.

He and his girl go on to the well. The other couple stay behind.

GEORGE (looking at the jalopy, amused):
What'll you use for tires when these are gone?

BOY:
Oh, it'll run much smoother on the rims.

George laughs, goes back to his *Variety*. The other couple see the headline:
STIX NIX HIX PIX

BOY (to girl):
I bet that's Greek talk.

GIRL:

> No. It's Swedish or Russian. (Repeats puzzledly.) Stix nix hix pix.

George lowers *Variety*, looks at the boy and girl, then laughs.

GEORGE:

> No—that's show business talk. Here, I'll translate it for you— (He puts his finger on each word in turn.) It means that the small towns don't like pictures about rubes. They want glamour—high-hat stuff.

The young couple glance at each other in surprise, then look back at George.

BOY:

> I thought it was jive talk.

GEORGE (puzzled):

> Jive which?

GIRL (eagerly):

> Are you an actor, sir?

GEORGE (modestly):

> Well—I used to be—in a way.

GIRL:

> What were some of your pictures?

George's "take" is very amusing.

GEORGE:

> I was on Broadway, young lady—the legitimate theater.[57]

152C. MED. THREE SHOT   ANOTHER ANGLE

GIRL:

> Oh . . . what is your name, sir?

GEORGE:

> Cohan . . . (Pauses for a reaction, but doesn't get it.) George M. Cohan.

The youngsters look at each other blankly, not recognizing the name. They shake their heads.

BOY:

> I guess you must've been before our time.

152D.  CLOSE-UP  GEORGE
He sits up a little, cocking one eyebrow defensively. Are those kids ribbing him? He tries to sound casual.

GEORGE:

> Didn't you ever see *Mary*? *Little Nellie Kelly*? *The Tavern*? *Ah, Wilderness*?

152E.  MED. THREE SHOT  FAVORING GEORGE
The young pair shake their heads.

GIRL:

> No, sir. Were you in them?

George looks at them suspiciously, unable to believe his ears.

GEORGE:

> Where were you kids brought up—in a vacuum bottle? (Then he smiles.) I'll bet your parents have seen me plenty of times.

BOY:

> They may have, but they don't talk about it.

GEORGE (he plays his ace):

> Do you remember a song called "Over There"?

The youngsters glance at each other, trying to recall it, but cannot.

GIRL:

> N-no, sir. Who sang it?

GEORGE (amazed and hurt):
> Who SANG IT!!?

BOY:
> Was it the theme song of something?

GEORGE (excitedly):
> You bet your life it was! Ten million—

BOY:
> Was that a follow-up to "Beat Me, Daddy, Eight to the Bar"?

GIRL:
> Or "Flat Foot Floogie with a Floy Floy"?

152F.     CLOSE-UP   GEORGE
He is speechless. All he can do is wince.

152G.     JALOPY
The couple at the car have finished pouring the water into the radiator.

BOY (calling out):
> Okay. She'll behave now.

152H.     GEORGE AND THE OTHER COUPLE

BOY:
> Well, we've got to scram now—swing session.

GIRL (to George):
> Thank you very much, Mr.—Mr.— What was your name again, sir?

COHAN (thoroughly deflated, his voice is barely audible):
> Cohan—

George starts slowly back toward the house. Off-scene the jalopy can be heard starting with rips and snorts.

DISSOLVE TO:

152I.   INT. FARMHOUSE   BEDROOM   GEORGE AND MARY
The startling discovery at the well is still irritating George's pride, but he tries to sound casual.

GEORGE:
> Can you imagine that? They'd never even heard of me!

MARY (tries to keep a straight face):
> But you've been away from the theater for years, George. A new generation has grown up since then. Naturally they don't remember you.

GEORGE (dissatisfied):
> Why not? On the Keith Circuit they remembered my mother and father for forty years!

MARY:
> That's because they were real troupers. They never had time to sit around an orchard and listen to their arteries harden.

GEORGE:
> What do you mean? There's nothing wrong with *my* arteries.

MARY (laughs):
> No—not right *now*—because those kids got you all worked up.

George cocks his head slightly to one side, eyeing her cagily.

GEORGE (slowly, suspiciously):
> Mary, you're trying to get a rise out of me for some reason. Come on—out with it.

152J.   MED. SHOT   GEORGE AND MARY
There is a tense moment's pause as they look at each other in the mirror, then Mary turns slowly to face him.

MARY:
I got a long distance call from Sam Harris this afternoon.

GEORGE:
Well, what about it?

MARY:
He's producing a new show by Kaufman and
Hart.[58]

GEORGE (puzzledly, as she pauses again):
They're good writers. I couldn't improve one of
their plays.

MARY:
Sam thinks you could—if you played the lead.

152K.   CLOSE-UP   GEORGE
His eyebrows cock in surprise, then he frowns firmly as
if annoyed.

GEORGE:
ME? No, sir! I've retired, and Sam knows it. The
*nerve* of that guy! What's he trying to do, spoil our
fun?

152L.   MED. SHOT   THE TWO

MARY (quietly):
But *are* you having fun, dear? (As he hesitates she
shakes her head.) When we were in Europe you
haunted every theater—not knowing a word that
was said on the stage—just to smell the greasepaint
again.

GEORGE (it's a good act):
Why, that's ridiculous! The only reason I see a show
now and then is—well—it keeps me out of the
night air. Fun? I'm having a *wonderful* time! To heck
with Broadway!

Mary isn't fooled by this at all. She sticks to her point with a wife's calm persistence and surgical skill.

MARY:
Sam said it's a great part and no other actor in the world but you could do it.

GEORGE (after a second):
Hmm—did he really say that?

MARY (nods):
Yes—and he needs you, George. He's in a spot. After all you've been to each other I think you ought to help him out—for old times' sake.

The CAMERA MOVES UP to George as he looks at her uncertainly for a moment, then steps closer to the mirror and looks at his face, moves the muscles this way and that, as if trying out an old instrument, while Mary watches eagerly, waiting for his decision. Finally he turns around.

GEORGE (with resignation):
Well, if Sam's in trouble—okay. Let's pack up.

With a happy cry, Mary jumps up and embraces him.

152M.  CLOSE SHOT  TWO  GEORGE AND MARY
with their arms around each other.

MARY (smiles):
I already have, darling! (George looks at her.) And I've got one more confession—I told Sam I'd try my best to talk you into it.

GEORGE (nods with a chuckle):
I knew you did, dear . . . I listened in on the downstairs phone.

Mary's mouth opens in amazement, then with a wife's amused indignation:

MARY:
> Why, you *devil!* You knew all the time!

GEORGE (nods, with a big grin):
> And now *I've* got a little confession, sweetheart
> . . . I called Sam back and told him I'd do the show.

Mary is utterly speechless. Then suddenly both of them burst out laughing and hug each other tightly.[59]

DISSOLVE TO:

152N.   FULL SHOT   A HUGE ELECTRIC SIGN ON
THEATER   (INSERT)
The biggest sign on Broadway, sparkling with a border of red, white, and blue lights, proclaims to the world:
SAM H. HARRIS PRESENTS
GEORGE M. COHAN
In his triumphal return to the stage
in
*I'd Rather Be Right*
The Greatest Musical Comedy Hit in Years

CAMERA PANS DOWN TO:

152O.   EMPTY LOBBY

CAMERA PANS OVER TO:

152P.   PICTURE OF GEORGE
pointing his finger in a pose from the show.

DISSOLVE TO:

152Q.   INT. THEATER   GEORGE
doing the "Off the Record" number on the stage. At the end of the number, amid the applause of the audience,

DISSOLVE TO:

153.   INT. PRESIDENT'S OFFICE   GEORGE AND PRESIDENT

GEORGE:
> . . . And then came your wire. I— (Stops suddenly,
> springs to his feet.) Gosh—I've got a lot of nerve,
> taking up your time with the story of my life. Why

didn't you stop me, Mr. President? Gosh, I'm sorry—[60]

PRESIDENT:

Why, I wanted to hear the story of your life. It has a direct bearing on my sending for you— (He reaches into his desk, takes out a box, opens it, holds up a medal.) Do you know what this is?

GEORGE (peering at it):

It's the Congressional Medal of Honor—

PRESIDENT (turning the medal over):

Let's see what the inscription says— (Reads.) "To George M. Cohan, for his contribution to the American spirit." I congratulate you, Mr. Cohan.[61]

154.  CLOSE-UP  GEORGE

He stares at the medal, then at the president and back at the medal, speechless. There are almost tears in his eyes.

PRESIDENT'S VOICE:

I understand you're the first person of your profession to receive this honor. You should be very proud.

GEORGE (beginning to come out of the daze):

Oh, I *am*, Mr. President—but I'm sort of flabbergasted! I—I don't know what to say! (He looks at the medal again.) Are you *sure* there hasn't been some mistake? (The president chuckles and nods.) But this medal's only for people who've given their *lives* to the country—or done something big. I'm just a song-and-dance man. Everybody knows that.

155.  REVERSE ANGLE  FAVORING THE PRESIDENT

He smiles with amusement, but also with genuine liking for his visitor's modesty, and shakes his head.

THE PRESIDENT (with quiet sincerity):
> A man may give his life to his country in many different ways, Mr. Cohan. And quite often he isn't the best judge of how much he *has* given. Your songs were a symbol of the American spirit. "Over There" was just as powerful a weapon as any cannon, as any battleship we had in the first world war. Today, we're all soldiers, we're all on the front. We need more songs to express America. I know you and your comrades will give them to us.

GEORGE (determinedly):
> Mr. President—I'm just going to begin to earn this medal— (Holds up the medal.) It's quite a thing.

PRESIDENT (smiling):
> Well, it's the best material we could find, what with priorities and all—

GEORGE:
> Good-bye, Mr. President— (Smiles faintly.) My mother thanks you, my father thanks you, my sister thanks you—and I thank you. (The president grins.) And don't worry about this country, Mr. President—where else in the world today could a plain guy like me sit down and talk things over with the head man?

THE PRESIDENT (quietly):
> Well, that's about as good a definition of America as any I've ever heard. (Taking George's hand.) Good-bye, Mr. Cohan—and good luck.

GEORGE:
> Good luck to you, sir.

He turns away and starts down the corridor.

156.   MED. TRUCKING SHOT   GEORGE   DOWN THE CORRIDOR
As George walks the Negro butler passes him, bearing several suitcases.

NEGRO BUTLER (to George):
   Mrs. Roosevelt—she's leaving for San Francisco—

George grins, walks on down the long corridor of the White House. He looks up at the portraits of all the great Americans of the past, hung along the walls. The CAMERA PULLS BACK with him, past the pictures of Washington, Jefferson, Franklin, Lincoln, Woodrow Wilson, and his shoulders straighten up serenely in their distinguished company. His steps become almost a strut.

157. STREET   OUTSIDE THE WHITE HOUSE
A company of soldiers is parading by. As they march they are singing "Over There." The people on the sidewalk cheer them and join in the song. As the music fills the air

                                             CUT TO:

158. GEORGE
coming out of the White House grounds. As he sees and hears the soldiers singing his song he stops short. He is so greatly affected that all he can do is stand and look. A man standing next to him is singing. He turns to George.

MAN (to George):
   You look like an old-timer. Don't you remember this song?

GEORGE (smiling queerly):
   It's—it's coming back to me now.[62]

He starts to sing with the soldiers. Singing, he unconsciously starts down the street in step with the soldiers. The words grow very loud and distinct—"AND WE WON'T COME BACK TILL IT'S *OVER, OVER THERE!*"

                                             FADE OUT

## THE END

# Notes to the Screenplay

1   Critics, the bane of Cohan's existence, are satirized early on here by the Epsteins. Two of them emerge from the opening night's performance of *I'd Rather Be Right* with this exchange:

FIRST CRITIC: I call it a hit. What'll your review say?

SECOND CRITIC: I like it, too. So, er, I guess I'll pan it.

FIRST CRITIC: Oh. (Laughing.) Well, that's logical.

SECOND CRITIC: My publisher resents Cohan impersonating the president of the United States. Says our young readers dream of being president.

FIRST CRITIC: "I'd rather be right than be president . . . " Cohan may find out he isn't either one.

2   This prologue to the meeting between George and the president is likely the invention of Julius and Philip Epstein. Revisions for the prologue are dated January 14, 1942, roughly two months after the start of filming. But additional revisions took place as well, especially for the scene set in George's dressing room. The changes were slight, enhancing the humor and underlining George's anxiety at being summoned by the president. Among those last-minute changes: In the film, Sam Harris reads the telegram aloud because George cannot locate his reading glasses, instead of Mary's reading it while the camera scans its message in an "insert." There is no insert. (As in the Introduction, I use the name George to refer to the character in the screenplay and film, and the name Cohan to refer to the man in real life.)

3   Buckner's original Screenplay and Outline opens with this scene of George approaching the White House at a late hour in a light drizzle of rain.

4   The first mention of George Cohan's name is thusly footnoted in Buckner's Screenplay and Outline: "DIALOGUE DIRECTOR NOTE: The name is correctly pronounced Co-hann, with the accent on the last syllable." According to John McCabe, however, Cohan always pronounced it *Co-en*, in the Jewish tradition. "He was the only one in his family to do so, and this is possibly derivative from his many intimate friendships with many Jews in the theatre, particularly his

much-loved only partner and sometime brother-in-law, Sam H. Harris" (*George M. Cohan*, p. 3).

5 Even the small, inconsequential "transition" scenes were revised or stretched out through improvisation during shooting, as evidenced by the brief conversation between the Negro butler and George. The butler's single line, "Will you follow me, please, sir?" is padded considerably in the filmed *Dandy*:

NEGRO BUTLER: Good evenin', Mr. Cohan.
GEORGE: Good evening.
NEGRO BUTLER: We've been expecting you.
GEORGE: Thank you.
NEGRO BUTLER: Why, your coat's wet. Didn't you come in the car?
GEORGE: No, I walked up from the station. Washington's a great town to walk in. I always get a kick out of it, rain or shine.

6 This interesting topical jibe at Eleanor Roosevelt's constant travels on behalf of one cause or another was discreetly omitted from the film. Doing so partly obscured the specific identity of the president for dramatic purposes and partly represented Warners' support of FDR and sensitivity to his feelings. A similar joke in scene 156 was also cut (the butler, carrying luggage, passes George in the White House corridor and remarks, "Mrs. Roosevelt—she's leaving for San Francisco").

7 Buckner's first draft contained at this point an odd remark by the president, who says that, after seeing the Four Cohans perform in Boston during his schoolboy days, "I left the theatre feeling socially useless."

8 George's visit with the president was probably shot in its entirety and then edited as a "frame." It was also probably one of the last scenes to be filmed. Although it was rewritten several times, the scene never strayed far from the spirit of Buckner's original draft, which was rooted so strongly in Cohan's recollections. Interestingly, although Warners guarded FDR's image in the script, the studio allowed the Epsteins to rib the opposition party, as the following exchange from the film indicates:

PRESIDENT: The *Herald Tribune* says that you make a better president in *I'd Rather Be Right* than I am.
GEORGE: Don't forget, that's a Republican newspaper.

9 George's voice-over narration was extensively revised after the Final script was approved, here as elsewhere in the story, probably during postproduction. The Epsteins (or Cagney, perhaps) gave the narration an added historical and nostalgic flavor in its final form

and developed it more as a narrative thread. Here George says, "It was in Providence, Rhode Island, on the Fourth of July. There weren't so many stars then in the flag or on the stage. But folks knew more were coming. They were optimistic, happy, and expectant. The beginning of the Horatio Alger Age . . . "

10 This backstage vignette of Jerry Cohan's vaudeville stint in Providence was expanded and revised slightly for shooting. Buckner's first draft contained one of his many labored quips about Cohan's native Providence, later cut at the song-and-dance man's insistence:

STAGE MANAGER: You can't run through Providence in *that* outfit—and with makeup on.

JERRY COHAN (wildly): Who *cares* about Providence!

11 The Epstein brothers even rewrote throwaway quips. Buckner's line here was "The Irish are two blocks up ahead, Mike—right in front of the police."

12 As another example of how the Epsteins smartened up the writing, Buckner's line here was, "Well, I didn't catch the name—but I think it's a boy."

13 The revised narration in the film:

GEORGE'S VOICE: I guess the first thing I ever had my fist on was the American flag. I hitched my wagon to thirty-eight stars. And thirteen stripes. You know, I was six or seven years old before I realized they weren't celebrating my birthday on the Fourth of July. Then my folks got a real break when my little sister, Josie, made her entrance. She grew to love show business just as she loved everybody and everything. We toured the kerosene circuit in a tank show called "Daniel Boone on the Trail." Everybody doubled in brass. Dad walloped the bass drum. For some reason they teamed me with a donkey. I was a good Democrat, even in those days. Mother and Josie threw out handbills. Their smiles would have sold tickets to wooden Indians. They kept putting new stars in the flag and the Cohans kept rushing out to meet them. We had jokes to match every cornfield. We sang at every milk station.

The montage here includes Little Josie singing a snatch of "Strolling through the Park One Day" and Little George doing his version of "Dancing Master." The narration continues, voice-over.

GEORGE'S VOICE: We trouped through depression and inflation. Part of the country's growing pains. We froze in winter and roasted in summer. But it was a good life. It's a lucky family that dances together every day. Eighteen ninety-one found our fortunes flat as a pancake. Then came a bolt from the blue. Jobs for the whole family in a play called *Peck's Bad Boy*. It opened in Brooklyn. The town was noted for its spirited audiences. Even before it had a ball team.

14 Scene 16 is not in the film. Various efforts were made in successive drafts to dramatize the education of Little George and Josie Cohan, but all were ultimately abandoned, and there is no mention of their schooling in the film. One of the more interesting efforts was a scene by Buckner in the Revised Temporary script in which Little George and Josie materialize in Syracuse with their winterwear and luggage. George has a note from his teacher in North Brookfield, Massachusetts, which reads: "Dear Mr. Cohan: It is absolutely impossible to teach this boy any more. He KNOWS it all."

15 The Revised Temporary script had a note at this point: "The purpose of these scenes is to establish clearly the warm family relation of the Four Cohans, working side by side, one for all and all with a great bond of love."

16 As noted elsewhere, Cohan was helpful in furnishing sheet music, dance steps, and old photographs for these vaudeville scenes. The brief glimpse of the Four Cohans in blackface in the film may have come from their well-known "Lively Bootblack" routine. There is no mention of this blackface vignette, however, in Buckner's notes or in any of the script drafts.

17 The business of George's falling off the ladder is not in the film. The *Peck's Bad Boy* scene underwent many revisions as the production evolved, evidently borrowing heavily from Cohan's reminiscences, for similar material cropped up in the Kerr-Brady stageplay.

18 One of Buckner's screenplays noted: "It is Mr. Cohan's wish to open this sequence with a brief shot of the Four Cohans on stage just before the curtain rises, hastily embracing and wishing each other good luck, a traditional custom of the family on opening night." Despite Cohan's wishes, this "brief shot" of the "traditional custom" does not appear in the film.

19 Cohan supplied the dialogue from *Peck's Bad Boy*:
SCHULTZ (muttering): Why do you do this to me?
COP: So! It's to jail you go, me boy.
JERRY: Ah, now. There, there now. Henry's not really a bad boy. He's just mischievous. That's all. Er, Mr. Schultz, I think that should take care of the damage. What do you think?

SCHULTZ: Yeh.

NELLIE: Henry, I want you to promise our friend, the cop, and Mr. Schultz, that from now on you'll always be a good boy.

GEORGE: I'll promise. But I can still lick any kid in town.

20 Apparently the Epsteins revised scenes 21–31 one more time during shooting. Little George was to emerge as less arrogant than in early drafts, more in a precocious vein. Cohan was obviously sensitive about the character of the boy, and it is interesting to see how he and the screenwriters, first Buckner and then the Epsteins, resolved the moral of the *Peck's Bad Boy* interlude to their satisfaction. Cohan's version follows:

JERRY: You see, son, friendships are the biggest asset in any man's life and, of course, the only way to create friendships is to make friends. But people will hate you if you go about the country exploding as you did in that theater this afternoon. Such antics are not only disrespectful to your family, but all those performers, stagehands, everybody connected, all think now that you're just a loud-mouthed, brazen, incorrigible kid. And as a matter of fact, you're nothing of the kind; you're just a sensitive, overanxious, ambitious, temperamental boy and you love your work to such an extent that you lose all sense of patience with yourself and everybody else when everything doesn't go to suit you around the theater. Now don't you think I've summed you up pretty well?

Buckner, in his Revised Temporary, took his cue from Cohan's version:

GEORGE (excitedly): WHAT! Have I got to go through this EVERY NIGHT!

JERRY: Not if you've got friends with you. As you grow up, you'll find that show business is full of hard knocks. The only thing that really counts is friendship. And you'll never make friends by talking the way you did this afternoon. They'll think you're just a loud-mouthed brazen nuisance. But we know that you're not like that—down deep inside. You're just a sensitive, overanxious, temperamental boy. You love your work to such an extent that you lose all sense of patience with yourself and everybody else when things don't go to suit you around a theater.

21 This is the fade-out line in Buckner's first draft. The Epsteins' rewritten scene (31) is dated December 2, 1941, in the Final script and

concludes with Jerry's spanking of George, one of their minor contributions to the scene.

22 Revised dialogue and narration over the vaudeville montage:

NELLIE: Who are Lewis and Clark, George?

GEORGE, AS A BOY: Acrobats? Look at the swell write-up we got in *The Clipper*.

NELLIE: Write-up? . . .

GEORGE'S VOICE: You'd find us wherever new states sprouted on the prairie. We played every town in America that had a theater. . . .

GEORGE, AS A BOY: Any mail for Mr. Cohan?

CLERK: Oh, no. Your father picked up his mail.

GEORGE, AS A BOY: I mean for George M. Cohan. . . .

GEORGE'S VOICE: The next ten years rushed by like a circus train. Dad seemed content with the sticks, but I was straining at the leash. . . .

SECOND CLERK: Here's your mail, Mr. Cohan.

GEORGE: Thanks. A couple of tickets for the show. . . .

GEORGE'S VOICE: We were playing stock in Buffalo. And being versatile, I was playing my mother's father.

The scene that follows, from a play called *The Professor's Wife*, was set by Buckner in his first draft in New York City, not in Buffalo, and called for George to be dressed in the latest sartorial elegance, not "playing my mother's father." Cohan's famous curtain speech ("My mother thanks you," etc.) was originally dramatized in this scene, which segued into a scene with Agnes Nolan, backstage, preparing to sing. Apropos of nothing, George calls Agnes "Mary." "Why do you call me Mary?" she asks. "I don't know," George replies, "you just *look* like a Mary—and it goes a lot better with Nolan than Agnes." The lyrics to her ensuing song, "Life's a Funny Proposition, after All," contain the word "die," which cued one of Buckner's jibes at Providence. The stage manager complained, "Die—DIE!—you can't use that word in a Keith theater!" George replied, "Then what do you call it—'Booked in Providence'?"

23 Additional dialogue is at the end of this scene, with George inviting Mary out for "a nice cold bottle and a bird." ("What's a cold bottle?" "Well, that's what we in show business call a piece o' pie and a glass o' milk.") It was most likely Cagney who added such touches as the tongue-clucking noise, the drawn-out business of stripping off his makeup and beard, the "pipperino" slang, and the act of stomping on his fake beard as if it is afire.

24  There is additional montage here. In his version of the script, Cohan noted the desirability of the vaudeville montage scenes in order "to show the schooling or training or whatever you wish to call it of the early days when a performer got the chance to really learn his business and develop a versatility that is certainly lacking in the present-day theater."

25  According to John McCabe, Cohan actually borrowed the gist of his famous curtain speech from Julius Tannen, a gifted mime from Chicago who later became a vaudeville monologist.

26  This transition sequence (scenes 41–52), highlighted by Mary's song, was extensively rewritten for the film. Among other changes, Mary's song became "The Warmest Baby in the Bunch" and the one she is supposed to sing (according to the stage manager) became "The Wedding of the Lily and the Rose."
    Narration followed at this point:

GEORGE'S VOICE: Oh, things were tough. But at least I was in New York. I had a trunk full of songs and playscripts and a heart full of confidence. I'm glad I had it.

PUBLISHER: I'm sorry, I can't use this, Cohan.

GEORGE: Youth needs confidence. I'd learned my job the hard way, all over the United States. And now guys who had never been past the corner cigar store were saying my stuff was no good. A kid had to believe in himself to buck that.

27  George has this self-conscious reply to Dietz and Goff in Buckner's early, heavy-handed Revised Temporary script: "Who—ME? Listen, I AM THE POPULAR TOUCH! (He looks at them with great pity.) You don't know it yet, but you've had your days, boys. The public's had enough of 'Nellie, the Sewing Machine Girl' and all the rest of that hoopskirt melodrama you've been dishing out for fifty years. They want new shows with new music and new faces—punch, laughs, speed!"

28  The film dialogue that follows (to the end of the scene) was probably written on the set. Thus, in the film it is George, not Mary, who expresses confidence in their prospects of success.

GEORGE: Come on now, Mary. Don't let a couple o' gilpins like that get under your skin. There's no sense in crying now.

MARY: Buffalo is such a beautiful city.

GEORGE: Is that what you're crying about?

MARY (sobbing): It's a beautiful city, but I hate to go back to it.

GEORGE: Don't worry, you won't have to. I'll show them yet. I'm gonna have my name posted and plastered up and down

Broadway until I'm as well known as Hood's Sasparilla. And if you'll stick along, we'll whip 'em to a standstill. We'll take 'em like Grant took Richmond.

MARY: I never really thought of leaving, George.

GEORGE: We'll make this whole theatrical business sit up and holler for help. That's what we'll do. They'll all hear from us. Every one of 'em. They'll all hear from us!

The postscript to the Dietz and Goff scene (57A–57E) is dated January 14, 1942, in the Final script. The first half (A and B) is not in the film, and the rest underwent another rewriting, as the dialogue above indicates.

29 The Epsteins revised the boardinghouse scene slightly during shooting. One of the changes was to give George the fade-out line. When Madame Bartholdi brags about being known as Venus on Wheels, he rejoins, "I always knew you weren't a cook!" Another of the changes was to eliminate the byplay involving the magician, as well as the business of the juggler hoarding the goulash. Curtiz may have filmed these latter bits and then decided to cut them.

30 The scene with Schwab remains relatively intact in the film, with one notable addition being S. Z. Sakall's whimsical ejaculation, "Women! Women! Little rose petals!" (after his speech ending "and a lot of girls" in scene 66). Interestingly, in a draft written by Buckner, George sings "I Want to Be a Popular Millionaire" (not "Dandy"), and George and Harris flip a coin to determine their billing status.

31 Buckner's Temporary script carries this note:

The exact routining of the numbers for this show is left to the specialists. But the following set-up is provided as a suggestion of order in presentation, and personal elements which should be included. Costume and staging data is available from Research.

At Mr. Cohan's suggestion, we open with a night scene on a pier, with a gangplank leading up to a ship that is preparing to sail. The chorus is all on shipboard, at the rails, men and women, and there is much gaiety. For 1903 this was a very remarkable stage-set, with a startling "special-effect" to come.

Down center of the stage Jerry Cohan, playing one of the principal parts, is addressing George, the sporty Yankee jockey. Their costumes and delivery of dialogue are very amusing, and the entire show moves with great speed—"the Cohan touch."

32 In Buckner's first draft it is Mary who sings "Give My Regards to Broadway" during *rehearsals* for *Little Johnny Jones*, and the three Cohans are in the cast of the show.

33 Buckner described the trick shot in his Temporary script: "Apart from its story interest, the purpose of this shot is largely historical. In 1903 it was the most daring and exciting trick that had ever been pulled on the New York stage, and started George M. Cohan's fame for providing surprises. . . . Suddenly a rocket zooms up from the little ship in the distance, arches gracefully up into the top of the stage and explodes like a brilliant scattering of stars. In the dark theater the effect is fascinating and thrilling."

34 The film shows Dietz and Goff standing in the back of the theater with Dietz upbraiding his partner with this payoff line: "That was your department!"

As late as the Revised Temporary script, a scene followed here (suggested by Cohan in his version) at an all-night "coffee pot" in which Sam Harris and all four Cohans anxiously await the reviews in early editions of the New York newspapers.

In one of the major structural changes from Final screenplay to film, scenes 109–10 (the three Cohans in the railroad waiting room) were moved up to this point in the narrative, followed by the montage of the reunited four Cohans. That segues into George and Mary and the singing of "Mary's a Grand Old Name."

35 In the film, this line opens the scene. Otherwise, this sequence (85–85A) is similar in the film, with one notable revision at the end (the film version: "Oh, George!" "Take that up an octave." "George!" "That's better!"). Earlier drafts were quite different, however. In the Revised Temporary, George sings "Mary" to Mary much later in the story, at the Cohan farmhouse after learning of his parents' impending retirement.

36 According to McCabe, Fay Templeton's remark about "the delights of bucolia" being only forty-five minutes from Broadway in New Rochelle was actually made to Cohan by T. Harold Forbes, an actor friend.

37 Cohan put these self-congratulatory words into Erlanger's mouth in his version of the script: "Listen, Fay, he's different. Brand new; speed, pep, no holes, no encores, plays right through the applause. All his songs consistent with the play, just as though they were part of the dialogue. He's a showman, he's box office. Of course, he's a pretty fresh young fellow, but I insist that he's got something."

38 George's meeting with Fay Templeton was revised substantially for the film. Among other changes, Fay actually sits down at the piano and plays a verse of "Mary." The biting sarcasm of the dialogue was heightened also. For example:

ERLANGER: You know, we were just talking about you, George. Miss Templeton's never seen your work.

GEORGE: Oh, been sick or in Europe? . . .

ERLANGER: Well, George, how would you like to do a play with one of the biggest stars in America?

GEORGE: What do you think I've been doing?

ERLANGER (laughing): You see what I mean, Fay? Isn't he a card?

TEMPLETON: Positively a riot.

39 This crucial scene between George and Mary remains substantially the same in the film, except for such minor but subtle improvements as the following additional dialogue: GEORGE: "Ham or bacon?" MARY: "Bacon." GEORGE: "Good. Ham makes me self-conscious." Later, George's offer to make Mary "leading lady—no options" is changed to the more affecting "leading lady, run of the play."

40 In the film the chorus sings "Forty-five Minutes from Broadway" after Fay Templeton sings "Mary" and before she sings "So Long, Mary."

Buckner's Revised Temporary script had a note about the shooting of this number: "Again, the routining of this show is left to the experts, and dependent upon the amount of footage found necessary. The spotting of good specialty dance might give a change of pace and variety to the montage, and the excellent music from this show is underscored throughout. The general effect to be achieved is one of speed, color, novelty, and high spirits—the trademark of all Cohan shows."

41 Instead of the following scene in the railroad station (see note 34), an encounter between Eddie Foy and George occurs at this point in the film. Not in the screenplay, it was taken partially from an account of their meeting described in the *Brooklyn Eagle* of December 23, 1907, which is among the clippings in Buckner's research file. Treated in briefer form in an earlier Buckner draft, the scene was evidently embroidered during shooting by Foy, Jr., and Cagney:

FOY: Look at this guy Cohan. He's got 'em lined up at the box office. I've never seen the guy. He's got his name all over the place. Look at that. "Cohan and Harris present *George Washington, Jr.*, starring the author and composer, George M. Cohan." I wonder what the M. is for. Oh, modesty!

STREET CLEANER: Hello, Mr. Foy!

FOY: How are yuh?

STREET CLEANER: Sure enjoyed your show last night.

FOY: Thank you.

STREET CLEANER: You always appear in the kind of stuff I like.

FOY: Thank you. That's very nice of you. "George M. Cohan and his royal family. Books and lyrics, music, and directed by George M. Cohan. Printed by Sam Dubinsky." That must be Cohan's alias. He certainly did give himself a billing, this George M. Cohan.

GEORGE: You don't have to memorize that one, kid. There's plenty more all over town.

FOY: I'd like to forget it. Say, mister, you connected with this turkey?

GEORGE: What makes you think it's a turkey? I hear it's pretty good.

FOY: It's a malicious rumor to gyp the public. Who is this guy Cohan? Where's he from? What is he, an upstart?

GEORGE: Oh, he's been through the mill. Played everything. Small time, big time, vaudeville, rep shows. Even followed dog acts.

FOY: Must've looked like an encore. Say, er, is he as good as Foy?

GEORGE: Who?

FOY: Foy. Foy. Eddie Foy. Oh, pardon me.

GEORGE: Pardon me. I didn't quite catch the name. Would you mind spraying it again?

FOY: Eddie Foy! The star that's got the big show down the street with a chorus of seventy.

GEORGE: Why, I thought they looked a little younger than that. I hear now that Cohan's in town, Foy is gonna retire.

FOY: Foy won't retire till he's ninety!

GEORGE: Is it gonna take him that long to discover he has no talent? Why, they tell me, when he tries to sing, the orchestra puts up umbrellas.

FOY: Tries to sing! Foy is a genius! He keeps his audience glued to the seats.

GEORGE: That's one way o' keeping them in the theater. Cohan does it with talent. Look, produces his own plays, writes his own books, lyrics and music, plays the leads, and he's a great dancer.

FOY: He dances, eh? When does he get time to practice?

GEORGE: When you write your own plays you don't have to practice. Cohan's done all right. He's given the world "Yankee Doodle Dandy." What's Foy done for his country?

FOY: He gave 'em seven kids.

GEORGE: Does he dance?

FOY: One o' the best.

GEORGE: When does he get time to practice?

FOY: Say, listen, young fella. My name's Eddie Foy.

GEORGE: I know it. I'm George M. Cohan.

FOY: Oh, so you're Cohan? Well, if I said anything accidental to make you mad, I want you to know I'm darn glad I did.

GEORGE: I don't blame yuh. I'd feel the same way if I were up against Cohan. What do you like to drink?

FOY: Oh, moxie—

GEORGE: I can supply it! The attraction inside is a whole lot bigger than I am. Come and see it when your show closes.

42 In the film George, not the entire family, sings this opening verse. The fleeting mention of the "Grand Old Flag" routine in the screenplay suggests either that the production number had already been filmed or that the Epstein brothers left its staging to the specialists. It is one of the more elaborate musical highlights and includes a black sharecropper who intones a verse of "The Battle Hymn of the Republic," shots of the Lincoln Memorial and soldiers marching off to war, a "democracy tableau" of workers united in defense of the nation, and snatches of "Dixie," "My Country Tis of Thee," "Auld Lang Syne," and "When Johnny Comes Marching Home." Buckner's Revised Screenplay suggested the staging of the finale: "The 'Grand Old Flag' number should be given the bigger production, with flags all over the stage. This is an excellent opportunity for special trick effects with the flags, which were mechanically impossible in the original version of the play."

43 The following voice-over dialogue, which so perfectly captures the "message" of Cohan's life as represented in the film, is practically a throwaway:

AUTOGRAPH HUNTER: Can I have your autograph. Mr. Cohan?

WOMAN: To what do you attribute your continued success, Mr. Cohan?

GEORGE: Oh, I'm an ordinary guy who knows what ordinary guys like to see . . . Front row center! The greatest show on earth. The people!

MARY: To the people. God bless them!

44 This reference to Fred is the only specific one to Fred Niblo, Jr., the husband of Josie Cohan and a vaudevillian who later became a motion picture screenwriter-director.

45 This scene (116–120) was rewritten extensively for the film. It opens with Nellie and Mary feeding chickens, not setting the table for a picnic. George is in the back chopping wood with Josie, not break-

ing twigs. Sam Harris and Jerry Cohan are not in the scene at the outset. George tells Josie that he has purchased a silk smoking jacket for his father's birthday present, not "practically nothing." Among the memorable dialogue changes are George's wistful comment to Josie, "One Cohan from Four Cohans leaves nothing," and George's kicker to the idea for a wedding march—"It'll pack the pews."

One chronological note here: Jerry Cohan retires in 1906 in the Revised Temporary script; the Final script (scene 115) implies that he retired after 1915. Thus, the character of Jerry Cohan got younger and retired later in life as the script evolved.

46 This letter is based on an actual letter George M. Cohan gave to his father on January 31, 1914, Jerry Cohan's sixty-sixth birthday. A copy of the letter is among Buckner's research notes. In the film the occasion is Jerry Cohan's sixty-second birthday.

47 This interior scene at the Cohan family farm, like the exterior scene that precedes it, was rewritten somewhat before shooting. Much of the content remains intact, but the subtlety and poignancy of the scene—especially of the presentation of George's gift to his father—are enhanced in the film.

48 The wording is slightly different in the film: "One success followed another. But there was one challenge I hadn't met. Critics kept saying that musicals and cheap comedies were all I could write. I could wave a flag, they said, and nothing else. So I wrote a legitimate drama, very deep and very significant. No music, no gags, no flag-waving. I called it *Popularity*. The title showed how hard I was hoping. I couldn't attend the opening performance because I was appearing down the street in *The Yankee Prince*."

49 Scenes 122–126, dated January 6, 1942, underwent additional revisions before shooting. Ultimately, the *Popularity* subplot became less self-conscious and more amusing. Revised dialogue:

GEORGE: These critics have been after my blood for years. They'll gang up on me and do a good job of it. But I'll beat 'em to it. I'll take an ad in every paper right alongside their reviews, telling the public we've got the greatest show in town, "an unqualified hit sold out for ten weeks in advance, will run a year." It'll be my word against theirs and the public'll believe me.

HARRIS: Aw, listen, Georgie, you can't do that—

GEORGE: Why not?

HARRIS: You've got too big a reputation. Listen, you can't disappoint the public. They'll never forgive you. They'll never trust you again. We stuck our necks out. We got clipped. Georgie! Listen, George, you can't do this. You'll always regret it.

GEORGE: Sit down and take this: "To the theater-going public. I wrote a play called *Popularity*. Mr. Harris and I produced that play. In the opinion of people we respect, it is a bad play. In this we heartily concur. It is a *very* bad play. I do humbly apologize and ask forgiveness for having presented anything of which you couldn't possibly approve. There will be five more performances. Please miss them. Signed—" Happy?

50 George has voice-over narration: "It seems it always happens. Whenever we get too high-hat and too sophisticated for flag-waving, some thug nation decides we're a pushover all ready to be blackjacked. And it isn't long before we're looking up, mighty anxiously, to be sure the flag's still waving over us."

51 The scene at the recruiting center is dated January 9, 1942, but was evidently rewritten extensively. In the film George is recognized by a sergeant who used to be a clerk at the Friar's Club; he gets rejected because of his advanced age (thirty-nine), not his flat feet; he does an energetic buck-and-wing to impress the recruiters with his vigor (declaring, "This war's a coffee klatch compared to a season with a musical show!"); and it is a military man, not a truck driver, who cues the song "Over There" (by saying to George, "Thank you very much for your entertainment, Mr. Cohan, but I'm afraid we have more need of you here than *over there*").

52 In the film "Over There" is sung not by a "beautifully dressed" Fay Templeton but by an anonymous singer (Frances Langford) dressed in military garb. Although not mentioned in the screenplay, the lights at the army camp do go out in this scene, just as Cohan had recollected such an incident in his conversations with Buckner.

53 Cohan noted in his version: "This shot of the boys marching away might possibly be a delicate thing to do considering world conditions today, but if it is strongly planted that it is June 1917, and *not* 1941, you might get away with it."

54 Instead, George narrates: "We'd won the world war. Manhattan went wild with postwar hysteria. But I spiked my shows with prewar stuff, the sentiment and humor an older America had aged in the wood." Toward the end of the montage that follows, George's voice is heard: "Still, it was lonely on the Main Stem. Mother and Josie were gone. Dad was by himself on the farm and had grown very old. Every night I went to the theater, I expected a phone call. Well, it finally came."

55 The death of Jerry Cohan does not occur in any previous draft of *Dandy*, and thus it can be credited to the Epsteins. It was rewritten only slightly for the film. Cohan does not weep in the Final script (that was Cagney's touch). Scene 148 is not in the film.

56 George narrates: "Life was less full, but it was by no means empty. I still had Mary, a playmate as well as a helpmate. We set out to rubberneck at the world." Dialogue follows during a montage of travel clips, including George's description of what yodeling is: "Nothing but hog calling with frost on it." Then George continues: "But folks always come back to where their heart is. So we came back to the farm, the farm we Cohans had dreamed of when farmers were envying us."

Scenes 152A–Q are dated January 13, 1942, making them among the last official changes to be incorporated into the Final script.

57 Considering Cohan's unpleasant experiences with movie-making, this exchange between George and the teen-ager is interesting. In the Revised Temporary script, the "STIX NIX HIX PIX" scene was set at the Cafe de la Paix in Paris, while George and Mary are traveling.

58 In Cohan's version, George is asked to star in *Ah, Wilderness!*, not a musical production written and scored (after all) by former rivals and nemeses. But Warners undoubtedly found the FDR musical to be more timely for the purposes of *Dandy*. Cohan has George discussing the offer with his friend and lawyer Cap O'Brien: "Listen, Cap, you know I've never gotten much real recognition as a legitimate actor here on Broadway. Being a sort of jack of all trades around the theater, the public's never taken me very seriously from an acting standpoint. They've got me tabbed as just a hoofer, a trick playwright, a flag waver and all that sort of thing. But even before I was fifteen years of age, don't forget that I played more parts in one season at Buffalo than the average Broadway actor plays in a lifetime. I had a real schooling, Cap, and I feel I'm a whole lot better trouper than the New York critics give me credit for being. And I'd just like to show those babies that I'm a pretty good actor and that I don't have to put on a pair of dancing shoes to prove it. Now here's my opportunity—this part in the O'Neill play."

59 A piece of Curtiz or Cagney stage business here plays off the serious tone of the preceding scene. As he backs away from Mary, George bumps his head on a post, mutters an ouch, and is good-naturedly kissed by Mary.

60 The revised line here evidences Cagney's tinkering, for he was a lifelong lover and quoter of poetry: "And then came your wire. I was really worried. Well, here I am, goin' on like Tennyson's 'Brook,' giving you the story of my life. I'm sorry. I didn't mean to do that. You should have stopped me."

61 Throughout the many drafts, this scene retained much of Buckner's (and Cohan's) content, albeit with minor structural and other changes. Among the lines that were dropped was this political reference, from an early Buckner draft, considered too sensitive by Warners: "For once," says FDR jovially, "Congress and I are in unanimous agreement, so please don't discourage us." Also, in the film George's medal reads, "To George M. Cohan for his contribution to the American Spirit, 'Over There' and 'Grand Old Flag.' Presented by Act of Congress."

62 In the film a soldier says to George, "What's the matter, old-timer? Don't you remember this song?" "It seems to me I do," replies George. "Well, I don't hear anything," says the soldier.

# Production Credits

| | |
|---|---|
| *Executive Producer* | Hal B. Wallis |
| *Associate Producer* | William Cagney |
| *Directed by* | Michael Curtiz |
| *Screenplay by* | Robert Buckner and Edmund Joseph (Julius J. and Philip G. Epstein) |
| *Original Story by* | Robert Buckner |
| *Lyrics and Music by* | George M. Cohan |
| *Musical Scoring* | Heinz Roemheld and Ray Heindorf |
| *Director of Photography* | James Wong Howe, A.S.C. |
| *Dialogue Director* | Hugh MacMullan |
| *Film Editor* | George Amy |
| *Art Director* | Carl Jules Weyl |
| *Montages by* | Don Siegel |
| *Dance Numbers Staged and Directed by* | Leroy Prinz and Seymour Felix |
| *James Cagney's Dances Routined by* | John Boyle |
| *Technical Advisor* | William Collier, Sr. |
| *Sound by* | Nathan Levinson |
| *Makeup Artist* | Perc Westmore |
| *Gowns by* | Milo Anderson |
| *Orchestral Arrangements* | Ray Heindorf |
| *Musical Director* | Leo F. Forbstein |

Running time: 126 minutes
Released: May 29, 1942

# Cast

| | |
|---:|:---|
| *George M. Cohan* | James Cagney |
| *Mary* | Joan Leslie |
| *Jerry Cohan* | Walter Huston |
| *Sam Harris* | Richard Whorf |
| *Fay Templeton* | Irene Manning |
| *Dietz* | George Tobias |
| *Nellie Cohan* | Rosemary DeCamp |
| *Josie Cohan* | Jeanne Cagney |
| *Singer* | Frances Langford |
| *Erlanger* | George Barbier |
| *Schwab* | S. Z. Sakall |
| *Theater Manager* | Walter Catlett |
| *George M. Cohan, age thirteen* | Douglas Croft |
| *Eddie Foy, Sr.* | Eddie Foy, Jr. |
| *Albee* | Minor Watson |
| *Goff* | Chester Clute |
| *Madame Bartholdi* | Odette Myrtil |
| *Josie Cohen, age twelve* | Patsy Lee Parsons |
| *The President* | Captain Jack Young |
| *Butler* | Clinton Rosamond |
| *Receptionist* | Audrey Long |
| *Stage Manager, Providence* | Spencer Charters |
| *Sister Act* | Dorothy Kelly, Marijo James |
| *George M. Cohan, age seven* | Henry Blair |
| *Josie Cohan, age six* | Jo Ann Marlow |
| *Stage Manager* | Thomas Jackson |
| *Fanny* | Phyllis Kennedy |
| *White House Guard* | Pat Flaherty |
| *Magician* | Leon Belasco |
| *Star Boarder* | Syd Saylor |
| *Stage Manager, New York* | William B. Davidson |
| *Dr. Llewellyn* | Harry Hayden |

## Cast

| | |
|---|---|
| *Dr. Anderson* | Francis Pierlot |
| *Teen-agers* | Charles Smith, Joyce Reynolds, Dick Chandlee, Joyce Horne |
| *Sergeant* | Frank Faylen |
| *Theodore Roosevelt* | Wallis Clark |
| *Betsy Ross* | Georgia Carroll |
| *Sally* | Joan Winfield |
| *Union Army Veterans* | Dick Wessel, James Flavin |
| *Schultz in* Peck's Bad Boy | Fred Kelsey |
| *Hotel Clerks* | George Meeker, Frank Mayo |
| *Actor, Railroad Station* | Tom Dugan |
| *Telegraph Operator* | Creighton Hale |
| *Wise Guy* | Murray Alper |
| *Army Clerk* | Garry Owen |
| *Nurse* | Ruth Robinson |
| *Reporters* | Eddie Acuff, Walter Brooke, Bill Edwards, William Hopper |
| *First Critic* | William Forrest |
| *Second Critic* | Ed Keane |
| *Girl* | Dolores Moran |
| *Chorus Girls in* Little Johnny Jones | Poppy Wilde, Lorraine Gettman (Leslie Brooks) |

This comprehensive cast list is from Homer Dickens, *The Films of James Cagney* (Secaucus, N.J.: Citadel Press, 1972), pp. 168–69.

# Appendix

Lyrics to the songs in *Yankee Doodle Dandy* follow. All the songs were composed by George M. Cohan, except for "All Aboard for Old Broadway" and "Off the Record" (see footnote 7 in the Introduction). Additional dialogue by the chorus for the production numbers "Yankee Doodle Dandy" and "You're a Grand Old Flag" is also given.

The Dancing Master

Larry O'Leary is me name.
By trade I am a dancing master.
And there's no one can teach the same
Nor teach it any faster.
It's easy, very easy,
If you watch ev'ry twist, ev'ry turn.
Keep your eyes upon me
And surprised you will be
At the dancing you have yet to learn.

© Copyright: George M. Cohan Music Publishing Co., Inc. Used by Permission.

I Was Born in Virginia

I was born in Virginia.
That's the state that will win yuh.
If you've got a soul in yuh,
Ain't no southerner town.
In the city of Norfolk,
Home of beauties and war talk,
Reckon you'll like it
If you should strike it
That doggone town.

© Copyright: George M. Cohan Music Publishing Co., Inc. Used by Permission.

*Appendix*

The Warmest Baby in the Bunch
When they see her comin'
All dem babies take a chill,
Diamonds glist'nin' all around
And style enough to kill,
Her steady fella broke a dice game
Down in Louisville,
And buys her chicken every day for lunch.
Come seben!
Dreamy eyes that sparkle
And she rolls them mighty cute,
Colored gent'man say that lady
Cert'ny is a bute,
Go broke, dat she's a hot potater,
She's a red hot radiator,
She's the warmest baby in the bunch.

Harrigan
Who is the man who will spend
Or will even lend?
Harrigan!
That's me!
Who is your friend,
When you find that you need a friend?
Harrigan!
That's me!
I'm just as proud of me name,
You see, as an emperor, czar,
Or a king could be.
Who is the man helps a man
Ev'ry time he can?
Harrigan!
That's me!
H-A-double R-I-G-A-N spells Harrigan
Proud of all the Irish blood that's in me,
And divil a man can say a word agin me.
H-A-double R-I-G-A-N you see
Is a name that a shame
Never has been connected with,
Harrigan, that's me!

[I'm a] Yankee Doodle Dandy

GEORGE:
I'm the kid that's all the candy,
I'm a Yankee Doodle Dandy,
I'm glad I am:

CHORUS:
So's Uncle Sam.

GEORGE:
I'm a real live Yankee Doodle,
Made my name and fame and boodle,
Just as Mr. Doodle did
By riding on a pony.
I love to listen to the Dixie strain,
I long to see the girl I left behind me;
That ain't a josh,
She's a Yankee, by gosh!

CHORUS:
Oh, say, can you see—

GEORGE:
Anything about a Yankee that's a phoney?

CHORUS:
Little Johnny Jones,
The jockey from the U.S.A.

GEORGE:
Will ride the pony Yankee Doodle
English derby day.

CHORUS:
Jonesy's broken records
Ev'ry track at ev'ry meet.

GEORGE:
So Yankee Doodle's gonna be the boy
They have to beat.

CHORUS:
Sportsmen of the British Isles
Who've followed his career,
Have offered Johnny anything
to keep him over here.

GEORGE:
But all the money in the
Bank of England couldn't pay
Enough to keep young Johnny Jones away
From old Broadway.

CHORUS:
If you want to take a tip,
The surest of sure things—
GEORGE:
Have your houses mortgaged,
Hock your watches,
Pawn your rings.
CHORUS:
And put it all on Yankee Doodle,
Johnny Jones is up!
GEORGE:
I'm gonna give America
The English derby cup!
CHORUS:
He's gonna give America
The English derby cup.
GEORGE:
I'm a Yankee Doodle Dandy,
A Yankee Doodle, do or die;
A real live nephew of my Uncle Sam,
Born on the Fourth of July.
I've got a Yankee Doodle sweetheart,
She's my Yankee Doodle joy.
Yankee Doodle came to London,
Just to ride the ponies,
I am that Yankee Doodle boy.
CHORUS:
He's a Yankee Doodle Dandy,
A Yankee Doodle, do or die;
A real live nephew of his Uncle Sam,
Born on the Fourth of July.
He's got a Yankee Doodle sweetheart,
She's his Yankee Doodle joy.
Yankee Doodle came to London,
Just to ride the ponies,
He is that Yankee Doodle boy.

## Appendix

### All Aboard for Old Broadway

All aboard, we'll soon be sailing for
The city of old New York.
Broadway nights, a million dancing lights,
Thrilling sights everywhere you go.
Londontown, we're bidding you adieu.
Gee, we hate to say good-bye to you.
All aboard. Good-bye to Londontown.
Hello to old Broadway.

### Give My Regards to Broadway

Give my regards to Broadway,
Remember me to Herald Square;
Tell all the gang at Forty-second Street
That I will soon be there.
Whisper of how I'm yearning
To mingle with the old time throng;
Give my regards to old Broadway
And say that I'll be there ere long.

© Copyright: George M. Cohan Music Publishing Co., Inc. Used by Permission.

### Barber's Ball

Everybody's goin' to the barber's ball
There ain't a-goin' to be any sleep at all
Until the stars are gone
Until the break of dawn.
We're gonna dance at the barber's ball.

© Copyright: George M. Cohan Music Publishing Co., Inc. Used by Permission.

### Mary

My mother's name was Mary.
She was so good and true.
Because her name was Mary
She called me Mary, too.
She wasn't gay or airy,
But plain as she could be.
I'd hate to meet a Mary
Who called herself Marie.

*Appendix*

For it is Mary, Mary,
Plain as any name can be.
But with propriety
Society will say Marie!
But it was Mary! Mary!
Long before the fashions came.
And there is something there
That sounds so square,
It's a grand old name.

Forty-five Minutes from Broadway
Only forty-five minutes from Broadway,
Think of the changes it brings,
For the short time it takes,
What a difference it makes,
In the ways of the people and things,
Oh, what a fine bunch of rubens,
Oh, what a jay atmosphere,
They have whiskers like hay,
And imagine Broadway,
Only forty-five minutes from here.

So Long, Mary

FAY:
It's awfully nice of all you boys
To see me to the train—
CHORUS:
So long, Mary!
FAY:
I didn't think you'd care
If you should ne'er see me again—
CHORUS:
You're wrong, Mary!
FAY:
This reminds me of my family,
On the day I left Schenectady,
To the depot then they came to me.

I seem to hear them say
"So long, Mary"
CHORUS:
Mary, we will miss you so.
FAY:
So long, Mary,
CHORUS:
How we hate to see you go.
FAY:
And we'll all be longing for you, Mary,
While you roam—
CHORUS:
So long, Mary,
Don't forget to come back home.

## You're a Grand Old Flag

GEORGE:
There's a feeling comes a-stealing,
And it sets my brain a-reeling.
When I listen to the music of a military band.
Every tune like "Yankee Doodle" simply sets me off my noodle,
It's that patriotic something that no one can understand.
BOYS:
Way down south in the land of cotton—
GEORGE:
Melody, untiring,
It's so inspiring—
BOYS:
Hurrah! Hurrah.
We'll join the jubilee.
GEORGE:
And that's going some
For the Yankees, by gum.
Red, white, and blue.
I am for you.
Honest, you're a grand old flag.
You're a grand old flag.
You're a high-flying flag.
And forever, in peace, may you wave.

You're the emblem of
The land I love.
GEORGE AND BOY SCOUTS:
The home of the free
And the brave.
GEORGE:
Ev'ry heart beats true,
Under red, white, and blue
Where there's never a boast or brag.
GEORGE AND BOY SCOUTS:
But should auld acquaintance be forgot,
Keep your eye on that grand old flag.
BOYS:
Rally 'round the flag.
Let us rally 'round the flag.
GEORGE:
We took the red from the flame of dawn. The dawn of a new nation.
And the white, with the white of the snow at Valley Forge. The blue
was the blue of the free open sky And the stars were the thirteen
sisters by the sea who built their home and called it liberty.
BOYS:
To symbolize our spirit—
GEORGE:
Right.
BOYS:
The spirit of freedom.
CHORUS:
We're one for all and all for one,
Behind the man, behind the gun.
And now that we're in it,
We're going to win it,
We can't lose a minute.
There's work to be done.
We're with 'em,
We're with 'em.
United we stand
In peace and war.
We're with 'em.
We're with 'em.
We'll fight as we did before.
For "my country 'tis of thee

Sweet land of liberty
Of thee we sing—"
You're a grand old flag,
You're a high-flyin' flag.
And forever, in peace, may you wave.
You're the emblem of
The land I love,
The home of the free and the brave.
Every heart beats true,
Under red, white, and blue.
Where there's never a boast or brag.
But should auld acquaintance be forgot—
Keep your eye on the grand old flag.
GEORGE:
Right again!
BOYS:
The spirit that gave birth
To American democracy.
GEORGE:
That's the spirit—
BOYS:
You're a grand old flag.
What a grand old flag!
BARITONE:
Glory, glory, hallelujah.
Glory, glory, hallelujah.
Glory, glory, hallelujah.
BARITONE AND CHORUS:
His truth goes marching on!
LINCOLN'S VOICE:
And that government of the people, by the people,
for the people shall not perish from the earth—
BOYS:
Johnny comes marching home again, hurrah! Hurrah!
We'll give him a hearty welcome then, hurrah!
Hurrah!
The men will cheer.
The boys will shout.
The ladies, they will all turn out.
And we'll all feel gay when Johnny comes marching home.

*Appendix*

Come along with Me Away
Like the wand'ring minstrel I just
Trudged along the way,
Wand'ring day by day,
No selection of direction,
Till I heard a lovely voice,
Which seemed to softly say:
"Come along with me,
Come along with me away."

© Copyright: George M. Cohan Music Publishing Co., Inc. Used by Permission.

Over There
Johnnie, get your gun, get your gun, get your gun,
Take it on the run, on the run, on the run.
Hear them calling you and me,
Ev'ry son of liberty.
Hurry right away,
No delay, go today,
Make your daddy glad to have had such a lad,
Tell your sweetheart not to pine—
To be proud her boy's in line.
Over there, over there,
Send the word, send the word over there
That the Yanks are coming,
The Yanks are coming,
The drums rum-tumming ev'rywhere.
So prepare, say a prayer,
Send the word, send the word to beware,
We'll be over,
We're coming over,
And we won't come back till it's over over there.

Copyright © 1917, renewed 1945 Leo Feist, Inc. All rights reserved. Used by
permission.

Nellie Kelly, I Love You
In a kingdom all our own
With little cupid on the throne,
With a prince and princess on my knee,
You'll be as happy as can be.

In a love nest, cozy and warm,
Like a doll's nest
Down on the farm.
And it's all day long they bring
Flowers all dripping with dew,
And they join the chorus of
Nellie Kelly, I love you.

### Off the Record

It's really a wonderful job,
For fellows like George, Abe, and me, too.
It's great to shake hands with the mob
And to hold every kid on your knee, too.
Every word that I speak goes into headlines,
When I speak all the papers hold their deadlines.
But I've found a way of dropping a hint.
Or a glint of the truth.
That the boys cannot print.
For instance, for instance—
When I was courting Eleanor,
I told her Uncle Teddy
I wouldn't run for president unless the job was steady.
Don't print it.
It's strictly off the record.

We entertained the royalty.
But we were never flustered.
We gave them Yankee hotdogs
With Coleman's English mustard.
Don't print it.
It's strictly off the record.
It's pleasant at the White House,
But I'll tell you how I feel,
The food is simply terrible,
Just sauerkraut and veal.
If Mrs. R. would stay at home
I'd get a decent meal.
But that's off the record.

When I go up to Hyde Park
It's not for just the ride there.
It's not that I like Hyde Park
But I love to park and hide there.
Don't print it.
It's strictly off the record.
I sit up in my study
Writing gags for Mr. Ickes
And insults for the gentlemen
Who'd love to slip him mickeys.
Don't print that.
It's off the record.

I scrapped the Prohibition Act
When we required a bracer.
And finished up the Boulder Dam
To give the boys a chaser.
Don't print it.
It's strictly off the record.

And for my friends in Washington
Who complain about the taxes,
Who cares as long as we can knock the ax out of the axis?
Don't print it.
It's strictly off the record.
I can't forget how Lafayette helped give us our first chance
To win our fight for liberty,
And now they've taken France.
We'll take it back from Hitler and put ants in his Jap pants.
And that's for the record!

# Inventory

The following materials from the Warner library of the Wisconsin Center for Film and Theater Research were used by McGilligan in preparing *Yankee Doodle Dandy* for the Wisconsin/Warner Bros. Screenplay Series:

Research notes, "Material on the Life of George M. Cohan," by Robert Buckner, April 4, 1941, 63 pages.

Screenplay, by Buckner, June 12, 1941, 88 pages. "Detailed Outline of Part Two," June 19, 1941, 29 pages.

Revised Screenplay, by Buckner, June 23, 1941, 88 pages. "Detailed Outline of Part Two," June 23, 1941, 30 pages.

Screenplay, by George M. Cohan, no date, annotated, 169 pages.

Revised Screenplay, by Buckner, September 30, 1941, 155 pages.

Temporary, by Buckner, October 16, 1941, 152 pages.

Revised Temporary, by Buckner, October 30, 1941, 171 pages.

Final, by Buckner and Julius and Philip Epstein, November 25, 1941, with revisions to January 14, 1942, 134 pages.

DESIGNED BY GARY GORE
COMPOSED BY GRAPHIC COMPOSITION, INC.
ATHENS, GEORGIA
MANUFACTURED BY FAIRFIELD GRAPHICS
FAIRFIELD, PENNSYLVANIA
TEXT AND DISPLAY LINES ARE SET IN PALATINO

Library of Congress Cataloging in Publication Data
Buckner, Robert.
Yankee Doodle Dandy.
(Wisconsin/Warner Bros. screenplay series)
Includes bibliographical references.
1. Cohen, George Michael, 1878–1949—Drama.
I. Joseph, Edmund, joint author.
II. Yankee Doodle Dandy. [Motion picture]    III. Series.
PN1997.Y322      791.43′72      80-52293
ISBN 0-299-08470-1
ISBN 0-299-08474-4 (pbk.)